DOVER EMPOWER YOUR LIFE SERIES

HOW TO
LIVE
ON
24 HOURS
A DAY

WITH
THE HUMAN MACHINE

ARNOLD BENNETT

D0897121

DOVER PUBLICATIONS, INC.
MINEOLA, NEW YORK

Bibliographical Note

This Dover edition, first published in 2007, is a republication of two works by Arnold Bennett: the 1910 Hodder & Stoughton (third) edition of *How to Live on Twenty-four Hours a Day,* originally published in 1908 by The New Age Press, London; and *The Human Machine* originally published in 1912 by The New Age Press, London.

International Standard Book Number: 0-486-45445-2

Manufactured in the United States of America
Dover Publications, Inc., 31 East 2nd Street, Mineola, N.Y. 11501

How to Live
on 24 Hours a Day

Contents

Preface

This preface, though placed at the beginning, as a preface must be, should be read at the end of the book.

I have received a large amount of correspondence concerning this small work, and many reviews of it—some of them nearly as long as the book itself—have been printed. But scarcely any of the comment has been adverse. Some people have objected to a frivolity of tone; but as the tone is not, in my opinion, at all frivolous, this objection did not impress me; and had no weightier reproach been put forward I might almost have been persuaded that the volume was flawless! A more serious stricture has, however, been offered—not in the press, but by sundry obviously sincere correspondents—and I must deal with it. A reference to page 21 will show that I anticipated and feared this disapprobation. The sentence against which protests have been made is as follows:—"In the majority of instances he [the typical man] does not precisely feel a passion for his business; at best he does not dislike it. He begins his business functions with some reluctance, as late as he can, and he ends them with joy, as early as he can. And his engines, while he is engaged in his business, are seldom at their full 'h.p.'"

I am assured, in accents of unmistakable sincerity, that there are many business men—not merely those in high positions or with fine prospects, but modest subordinates with no hope of ever being much better off—who do enjoy their business functions, who do not shirk them, who do not arrive at the office as late as possible and depart as early as possible, who, in a word, put the whole of their force into their day's work and are genuinely fatigued at the end thereof.

5

I am ready to believe it. I do believe it. I know it. I always knew it. Both in London and in the provinces it has been my lot to spend long years in subordinate situations of business; and the fact did not escape me that a certain proportion of my peers showed what amounted to an honest passion for their duties, and that while engaged in those duties they were really *living* to the fullest extent of which they were capable. But I remain convinced that these fortunate and happy individuals (happier perhaps than they guessed) did not and do not constitute a majority, or anything like a majority. I remain convinced that the majority of decent average conscientious men of business (men with aspirations and ideals) do not as a rule go home of a night genuinely tired. I remain convinced that they put not as much but as little of themselves as they conscientiously can into the earning of a livelihood, and that their vocation bores rather than interests them.

Nevertheless, I admit that the minority is of sufficient importance to merit attention, and that I ought not to have ignored it so completely as I did do. The whole difficulty of the hard-working minority was put in a single colloquial sentence by one of my correspondents. He wrote: "I am just as keen as anyone on doing something to 'exceed my programme,' but allow me to tell you that when I get home at six thirty p.m. I am not anything like so fresh as you seem to imagine."

Now I must point out that the case of the minority, who throw themselves with passion and gusto into their daily business task, is infinitely less deplorable than the case of the majority, who go half-heartedly and feebly through their official day. The former are less in need of advice "how to live." At any rate during their official day of, say, eight hours they are really alive; their engines are giving the full indicated "h.p." The other eight working hours of their day may be badly organised, or even frittered away; but it is less disastrous to waste eight hours a day than sixteen hours a day; it is better to have lived a bit than never to have lived at all. The real tragedy is the tragedy of the man who is braced to effort neither in the office nor out of it, and to this man this book is primarily addressed. "But," says the other and more fortunate man, "although my ordinary programme is bigger than his, I want to exceed my programme too! I am living a bit; I want to live more. But I really can't do another day's work on the top of my official day."

The fact is, I, the author, ought to have foreseen that I should appeal most strongly to those who already had an interest in existence. It is always the man who has tasted life who demands more of it. And it is always the man who never gets out of bed who is the most difficult to rouse.

Well, you of the minority, let us assume that the intensity of your daily money-getting will not allow you to carry out quite all the suggestions in the following pages. Some of the suggestions may yet stand. I admit that you may not be able to use the time spent on the journey home at night; but the suggestion for the journey to the office in the morning is as practicable for you as for anybody. And that weekly interval of forty hours, from Saturday to Monday, is yours just as much as the other man's, though a slight accumulation of fatigue may prevent you from employing the whole of your "h.p." upon it. There remains, then, the important portion of the three or more evenings a week. You tell me flatly that you are too tired to do anything outside your programme at night. In reply to which I tell you flatly that if your ordinary day's work is thus exhausting, then the balance of your life is wrong and must be adjusted. A man's powers ought not to be monopolised by his ordinary day's work. What, then, is to be done?

The obvious thing to do is to circumvent your ardour for your ordinary day's work by a ruse. Employ your engines in something beyond the programme before, and not after, you employ them on the programme itself. Briefly, get up earlier in the morning. You say you cannot. You say it is impossible for you to go earlier to bed of a night—to do so would upset the entire household. I do not think it is quite impossible to go to bed earlier at night. I think that if you persist in rising earlier, and the consequence is insufficiency of sleep, you will soon find a way of going to bed earlier. But my impression is that the consequence of rising earlier will not be an insufficiency of sleep. My impression, growing stronger every year, is that sleep is partly a matter of habit—and of slackness. I am convinced that most people sleep as long as they do because they are at a loss for any other diversion. How much sleep do you think is daily obtained by the powerful healthy man who daily rattles up your street in charge of Carter Paterson's van? I have consulted a doctor on this point. He is a doctor who for twenty-four years has had a large general practice in a large flourishing suburb of London, inhabited by exactly such people as you and me. He is a curt man, and his answer was curt:

"Most people sleep themselves stupid."

He went on to give his opinion that nine men out of ten would have better health and more fun out of life if they spent less time in bed.

Other doctors have confirmed this judgment, which, of course, does not apply to growing youths.

Rise an hour, an hour and a half, or even two hours earlier; and—if you must—retire earlier when you can. In the matter of exceeding programmes, you will accomplish as much in one morning hour as in two evening hours. "But," you say, "I couldn't begin without some food, and servants." Surely, my dear sir, in an age when an excellent spirit-lamp (including a saucepan) can be bought for less than a shilling, you are not going to allow your highest welfare to depend upon the precarious immediate co-operation of a fellow creature! Instruct the fellow creature, whoever she may be, at night. Tell her to put a tray in a suitable position over night. On that tray two biscuits, a cup and saucer, a box of matches and a spirit-lamp; on the lamp, the saucepan; on the saucepan, the lid—but turned the wrong way up; on the reversed lid, the small teapot, containing a minute quantity of tea leaves. You will then have to strike a match—that is all. In three minutes the water boils, and you pour it into the teapot (which is already warm). In three more minutes the tea is infused. You can begin your day while drinking it. These details may seem trivial to the foolish, but to the thoughtful they will not seem trivial. The proper, wise balancing of one's whole life may depend upon the feasibility of a cup of tea at an unusual hour.

A. B.

I

THE DAILY MIRACLE

"Yes, he's one of those men that don't know how to manage. Good situation. Regular income. Quite enough for luxuries as well as needs. Not really extravagant. And yet the fellow's always in difficulties. Somehow he gets nothing out of his money. Excellent flat—half empty! Always looks as if he'd had the brokers in. New suit—old hat! Magnificent necktie—baggy trousers! Asks you to dinner: cut glass—bad mutton, or Turkish coffee—cracked cup! He can't understand it. Explanation simply is that he fritters his income away. Wish I had the half of it! I'd show him——"

So we have most of us criticised, at one time or another, in our superior way.

We are nearly all chancellors of the exchequer: it is the pride of the moment. Newspapers are full of articles explaining how to live on such-and-such a sum, and these articles provoke a correspondence whose violence proves the interest they excite. Recently, in a daily organ, a battle raged round the question whether a woman can exist nicely in the country on £85 a year. I have seen an essay, "How to live on eight shillings a week." But I have never seen an essay, "How to live on twenty-four hours a day." Yet it has been said that time is money. That proverb understates the case. Time is a great deal more than money. If you have time you can obtain money—usually. But though you have the wealth of a cloak-room attendant at the Carlton Hotel, you cannot buy yourself a minute more time than I have, or the cat by the fire has.

Philosophers have explained space. They have not explained time. It is the inexplicable raw material of everything. With it, all is possible; without it, nothing. The supply of time is truly a daily miracle, an affair genuinely astonishing when one examines it. You wake up in the morning, and lo! your purse is magically filled with twenty-four hours of the unmanufactured tissue of the universe of your life! It is yours. It is the most precious of possessions. A highly singular commodity, showered upon you in a manner as singular as the commodity itself!

For remark! No one can take it from you. It is unstealable. And no one receives either more or less than you receive.

Talk about an ideal democracy! In the realm of time there is no aristocracy of wealth, and no aristocracy of intellect. Genius is never rewarded by even an extra hour a day. And there is no punishment. Waste your infinitely precious commodity as much as you will, and the supply will never be withheld from you. No mysterious power will say:—"This man is a fool, if not a knave. He does not deserve time; he shall be cut off at the meter." It is more certain than consols, and payment of income is not affected by Sundays. Moreover, you cannot draw on the future. Impossible to get into debt! You can only waste the passing moment. You cannot waste to-morrow; it is kept for you. You cannot waste the next hour; it is kept for you.

I said the affair was a miracle. Is it not?

You have to live on this twenty-four hours of daily time. Out of it you have to spin health, pleasure, money, content, respect, and the evolution of your immortal soul. Its right use, its most effective use, is a matter of the highest urgency and of the most thrilling actuality. All depends on that. Your happiness—the elusive prize that you are all clutching for, my friends!—depends on that. Strange that the newspapers, so enterprising and up-to-date as they are, are not full of "How to live on a given income of time," instead of "How to live on a given income of money"! Money is far commoner than time. When one reflects, one perceives that money is just about the commonest thing there is. It encumbers the earth in gross heaps.

If one can't contrive to live on a certain income of money, one earns a little more—or steals it, or advertises for it. One doesn't necessarily muddle one's life because one can't quite manage on a thousand pounds a year; one braces the muscles and makes it guineas, and balances the budget. But if one cannot arrange that an income of twenty-four hours a day shall exactly cover all proper items of expenditure, one does muddle one's life definitely. The supply of time, though gloriously regular, is cruelly restricted.

Which of us lives on twenty-four hours a day? And when I say "lives," I do not mean exists, nor "muddles through." Which of us is free from that uneasy feeling that the "great spending departments" of his daily life are not managed as they ought to be? Which of us is quite sure that his fine suit is not surmounted by a shameful hat, or that in attending to the crockery he has forgotten the quality of the food? Which of us is not saying to himself—which of us has not been saying to himself all his life: "I shall alter that when I have a little more time"?

We never shall have any more time. We have, and we have always had, all the time there is. It is the realisation of this profound and neglected truth (which, by the way, I have not discovered) that has led me to the minute practical examination of daily time-expenditure.

II

The Desire to Exceed
One's Programme

"But," someone may remark, with fine English disregard of everything except the point, "what is he driving at with his twenty-four hours a day? I have no difficulty in living on twenty-four hours a day. I do all that I want to do, and still find time to go in for newspaper competitions. Surely it is a simple affair, knowing that one has only twenty-four hours a day, to content one's self with twenty-four hours a day!"

To you, my dear sir, I present my excuses and apologies. You are precisely the man that I have been wishing to meet for about forty years. Will you kindly send me your name and address, and state your charge for telling me how you do it? Instead of me talking to you, you ought to be talking to me. Please come forward. That you exist, I am convinced, and that I have not yet encountered you is my loss. Meanwhile, until you appear, I will continue to chat with my companions in distress—that innumerable band of souls who are haunted, more or less painfully, by the feeling that the years slip by, and slip by, and slip by, and that they have not yet been able to get their lives into proper working order.

If we analyse that feeling, we shall perceive it to be, primarily, one of uneasiness, of expectation, of looking forward, of aspiration. It is a source of constant discomfort, for it behaves like a skeleton at the feast of all our enjoyments. We go to the theatre and laugh; but between the acts it raises a skinny finger at us.

13

We rush violently for the last train, and while we are cooling a long age on the platform waiting for the last train, it promenades its bones up and down by our side and inquires: "O man, what hast thou done with thy youth? What art thou doing with thine age?" You may urge that this feeling of continuous looking forward, of aspiration, is part of life itself, and inseparable from life itself. True!

But there are degrees. A man may desire to go to Mecca. His conscience tells him that he ought to go to Mecca. He fares forth, either by the aid of Cook's, or unassisted; he may probably never reach Mecca; he may drown before he gets to Port Said; he may perish ingloriously on the coast of the Red Sea; his desire may remain eternally frustrate. Unfulfilled aspiration may always trouble him. But he will not be tormented in the same way as the man who, desiring to reach Mecca, and harried by the desire to reach Mecca, never leaves Brixton.

It is something to have left Brixton. Most of us have not left Brixton. We have not even taken a cab to Ludgate Circus and inquired from Cook's the price of a conducted tour. And our excuse to ourselves is that there are only twenty-four hours in the day.

If we further analyse our vague, uneasy aspiration, we shall, I think, see that it springs from a fixed idea that we ought to do something in addition to those things which we are loyally and morally obliged to do. We are obliged, by various codes written and unwritten, to maintain ourselves and our families (if any) in health and comfort, to pay our debts, to save, to increase our prosperity by increasing our efficiency. A task sufficiently difficult! A task which very few of us achieve! A task often beyond our skill! Yet, if we succeed in it, as we sometimes do, we are not satisfied; the skeleton is still with us.

And even when we realise that the task is beyond our skill, that our powers cannot cope with it, we feel that we should be less discontented if we gave to our powers, already overtaxed, something still further to do.

And such is, indeed, the fact. The wish to accomplish something outside their formal programme is common to all men who in the course of evolution have risen past a certain level.

Until an effort is made to satisfy that wish, the sense of uneasy waiting for something to start which has not started will remain to disturb the peace of the soul. That wish has been called by many names. It is one form of the universal desire for knowledge. And it is so strong that men whose whole lives have been given to the systematic acquirement of knowledge have been driven by it to overstep the limits of their programme in search of still more knowledge. Even Herbert Spencer, in my opinion the greatest mind that ever lived, was often forced by it into agreeable little backwaters of inquiry.

I imagine that in the majority of people who are conscious of the wish to live—that is to say, people who have intellectual curiosity—the aspiration to exceed formal programmes takes a literary shape. They would like to embark on a course of reading. Decidedly the British people are becoming more and more literary. But I would point out that literature by no means comprises the whole field of knowledge, and that the disturbing thirst to improve one's self—to increase one's knowledge—may well be slaked quite apart from literature. With the various ways of slaking I shall deal later. Here I merely point out to those who have no natural sympathy with literature that literature is not the only well.

III

Precautions Before Beginning

Now that I have succeeded (if succeeded I have) in persuading you to admit to yourself that you are constantly haunted by a suppressed dissatisfaction with your own arrangement of your daily life; and that the primal cause of that inconvenient dissatisfaction is the feeling that you are every day leaving undone something which you would like to do, and which, indeed, you are always hoping to do when you have "more time"; and now that I have drawn your attention to the glaring, dazzling truth that you never will have "more time," since you already have all the time there is— you expect me to let you into some wonderful secret by which you may at any rate approach the ideal of a perfect arrangement of the day, and by which, therefore, that haunting, unpleasant, daily disappointment of things left undone will be got rid of!

I have found no such wonderful secret. Nor do I expect to find it, nor do I expect that anyone else will ever find it. It is undiscovered. When you first began to gather my drift, perhaps there was a resurrection of hope in your breast. Perhaps you said to yourself, "This man will show me an easy, unfatiguing way of doing what I have so long in vain wished to do." Alas, no! The fact is that there is no easy way, no royal road. The path to Mecca is extremely hard and stony, and the worst of it is that you never quite get there after all.

The most important preliminary to the task of arranging one's life so that one may live fully and comfortably within one's daily budget of twenty-four hours is the calm realisation of the

17

extreme difficulty of the task, of the sacrifices and the endless effort which it demands. I cannot too strongly insist on this.

If you imagine that you will be able to achieve your ideal by ingeniously planning out a time-table with a pen on a piece of paper, you had better give up hope at once. If you are not prepared for discouragements and disillusions; if you will not be content with a small result for a big effort, then do not begin. Lie down again and resume the uneasy doze which you call your existence.

It is very sad, is it not, very depressing and sombre? And yet I think it is rather fine, too, this necessity for the tense bracing of the will before anything worth doing can be done. I rather like it myself. I feel it to be the chief thing that differentiates me from the cat by the fire.

"Well," you say, "assume that I am braced for the battle. Assume that I have carefully weighed and comprehended your ponderous remarks; how do I begin?" Dear sir, you simply begin. There is no magic method of beginning. If a man standing on the edge of a swimming-bath and wanting to jump into the cold water should ask you, "How do I begin to jump?" you would merely reply, "Just jump. Take hold of your nerves, and jump."

As I have previously said, the chief beauty about the constant supply of time is that you cannot waste it in advance. The next year, the next day, the next hour are lying ready for you, as perfect, as unspoilt, as if you had never wasted or misapplied a single moment in all your career. Which fact is very gratifying and reassuring. You can turn over a new leaf every hour if you choose. Therefore no object is served in waiting till next week, or even until to-morrow. You may fancy that the water will be warmer next week. It won't. It will be colder.

But before you begin, let me murmur a few words of warning in your private ear.

Let me principally warn you against your own ardour. Ardour in well-doing is a misleading and a treacherous thing. It cries out loudly for employment; you can't satisfy it at first; it wants more and more; it is eager to move mountains and divert the course of rivers. It isn't content till it perspires. And then, too often, when it feels the perspiration on its brow, it wearies all of a sudden and dies, without even putting itself to the trouble of saying, "I've had enough of this."

Beware of undertaking too much at the start. Be content with quite a little. Allow for accidents. Allow for human nature, especially your own.

A failure or so, in itself, would not matter, if it did not incur a loss of self-esteem and of self-confidence. But just as nothing succeeds like success, so nothing fails like failure. Most people who are ruined are ruined by attempting too much. Therefore, in setting out on the immense enterprise of living fully and comfortably within the narrow limits of twenty-four hours a day, let us avoid at any cost the risk of an early failure. I will not agree that, in this business at any rate, a glorious failure is better than a petty success. I am all for the petty success. A glorious failure leads to nothing; a petty success may lead to a success that is not petty.

So let us begin to examine the budget of the day's time. You say your day is already full to overflowing. How? You actually spend in earning your livelihood—how much? Seven hours, on the average? And in actual sleep, seven? I will add two hours, and be generous. And I will defy you to account to me on the spur of the moment for the other eight hours.

IV

The Cause of the Trouble

In order to come to grips at once with the question of time-expenditure in all its actuality, I must choose an individual case for examination. I can only deal with one case, and that case cannot be the average case, because there is no such case as the average case, just as there is no such man as the average man. Every man and every man's case is special.

But if I take the case of a Londoner who works in an office, whose office hours are from ten to six, and who spends fifty minutes morning and night in travelling between his house door and his office door, I shall have got as near to the average as facts permit. There are men who have to work longer for a living, but there are others who do not have to work so long.

Fortunately the financial side of existence does not interest us here; for our present purpose the clerk at a pound a week is exactly as well off as the millionaire in Carlton House-terrace.

Now the great and profound mistake which my typical man makes in regard to his day is a mistake of general attitude, a mistake which vitiates and weakens two-thirds of his energies and interests. In the majority of instances he does not precisely feel a passion for his business; at best he does not dislike it. He begins his business functions with reluctance, as late as he can, and he ends them with joy, as early as he can. And his engines while he is engaged in his business are seldom at their full "h.p." (I know that I shall be accused by angry readers of traducing the city worker; but I am pretty thoroughly acquainted with the City, and I stick to what I say.)

21

Yet in spite of all this he persists in looking upon those hours from ten to six as "the day," to which the ten hours preceding them and the six hours following them are nothing but a prologue and epilogue. Such an attitude, unconscious though it be, of course kills his interest in the odd sixteen hours, with the result that, even if he does not waste them, he does not count them; he regards them simply as margin.

This general attitude is utterly illogical and unhealthy, since it formally gives the central prominence to a patch of time and a bunch of activities which the man's one idea is to "get through" and have "done with." If a man makes two-thirds of his existence subservient to one-third, for which admittedly he has no absolutely feverish zest, how can he hope to live fully and completely? He cannot.

If my typical man wishes to live fully and completely he must, in his mind, arrange a day within a day. And this inner day, a Chinese box in a larger Chinese box, must begin at 6 P.M. and end at 10 A.M. It is a day of sixteen hours; and during all these sixteen hours he has nothing whatever to do but cultivate his body and his soul and his fellow men. During those sixteen hours he is free; he is not a wage-earner; he is not preoccupied by monetary cares; he is just as good as a man with a private income. This must be his attitude. And his attitude is all important. His success in life (much more important than the amount of estate upon what his executors will have to pay estate duty) depends on it.

What? You say that full energy given to those sixteen hours will lessen the value of the business eight? Not so. On the contrary, it will assuredly increase the value of the business eight. One of the chief things which my typical man has to learn is that the mental faculties are capable of a continuous hard activity; they do not tire like an arm or a leg. All they want is change—not rest, except in sleep.

I shall now examine the typical man's current method of employing the sixteen hours that are entirely his, beginning with his uprising. I will merely indicate things which he does and which I think he ought not to do, postponing my suggestions for "planting" the times which I shall have cleared—as a settler clears spaces in a forest.

In justice to him I must say that he wastes very little time before he leaves the house in the morning at 9.10. In too many houses he gets up at nine, breakfasts between 9.7 and 9.9½, and then bolts. But immediately he bangs the front door his mental faculties, which are tireless, become idle. He walks to the station in a condition of mental coma. Arrived there, he usually has to wait for the train. On hundreds of suburban stations every morning you see men calmly strolling up and down platforms while railway companies unblushingly rob them of time, which is more than money. Hundreds of thousands of hours are thus lost every day simply because my typical man thinks so little of time that it has never occurred to him to take quite easy precautions against the risk of its loss.

He has a solid coin of time to spend every day—call it a sovereign. He must get change for it, and in getting change he is content to lose heavily.

Supposing that in selling him a ticket the company said, "We will change you a sovereign, but we shall charge you three half-pence for doing so," what would my typical man exclaim? Yet that is the equivalent of what the company does when it robs him of five minutes twice a day.

You say I am dealing with minutiæ. I am. And later on I will justify myself.

Now will you kindly buy your paper and step into the train?

V

TENNIS AND THE IMMORTAL SOUL

You get into the morning train with your newspaper, and you calmly and majestically give yourself up to your newspaper. You do not hurry. You know you have at least half an hour of security in front of you. As your glance lingers idly at the advertisements of shipping and of songs on the outer pages, your air is the air of a leisured man, wealthy in time, of a man from some planet where there are a hundred and twenty-four hours a day instead of twenty-four. I am an impassioned reader of newspapers. I read five English and two French dailies, and the newsagents alone know how many weeklies, regularly. I am obliged to mention this personal fact lest I should be accused of a prejudice against newspapers when I say that I object to the reading of newspapers in the morning train. Newspapers are produced with rapidity, to be read with rapidity. There is no place in my daily programme for newspapers. I read them as I may in odd moments. But I do read them. The idea of devoting to them thirty or forty consecutive minutes of wonderful solitude (for nowhere can one more perfectly immerse one's self in one's self than in a compartment full of silent, withdrawn, smoking males) is to me repugnant. I cannot possibly allow you to scatter priceless pearls of time with such Oriental lavishness. You are not the Shah of time. Let me respectfully remind you that you have no more time than I have. No newspaper reading in trains! I have already "put by" about three-quarters of an hour for use.

Now you reach your office. And I abandon you there till six o'clock. I am aware that you have nominally an hour (often in reality an hour and a half) in the midst of the day, less than half of which time is given to eating. But I will leave you all that to spend as you choose. You may read your newspapers then.

I meet you again as you emerge from your office. You are pale and tired. At any rate, your wife says you are pale, and you give her to understand that you are tired. During the journey home you have been gradually working up the tired feeling. The tired feeling hangs heavy over the mighty suburbs of London like a virtuous and melancholy cloud, particularly in winter. You don't eat immediately on your arrival home. But in about an hour or so you feel as if you could sit up and take a little nourishment. And you do. Then you smoke, seriously; you see friends; you potter; you play cards; you flirt with a book; you note that old age is creeping on; you take a stroll; you caress the piano. . . . By Jove! a quarter past eleven. Time to think about going to bed! You then devote quite forty minutes to thinking about going to bed; and it is conceivable that you are acquainted with a genuinely good whisky. At last you go to bed, exhausted by the day's work. Six hours, probably more, have gone since you left the office—gone like a dream, gone like magic, unaccountably gone!

That is a fair sample case. But you say: "It's all very well for you to talk. A man *is* tired. A man must see his friends. He can't always be on the stretch." Just so. But when you arrange to go to the theatre (especially with a pretty woman) what happens? You rush to the suburbs; you spare no toil to make yourself glorious in fine raiment; you rush back to town in another train; you keep yourself on the stretch for four hours, if not five; you take her home; you take yourself home. You don't spend three-quarters of an hour in "thinking about" going to bed. You go. Friends and fatigue have equally been forgotten, and the evening has seemed so exquisitely long (or perhaps too short)! And do you remember that time when you were persuaded to sing in the chorus of the amateur operatic society, and slaved two hours every other night for three months? Can you deny that when you have something definite to look forward to at eventide, something that is to employ all your energy—the thought of that something gives a glow and a more intense vitality to the whole day?

What I suggest is that at six o'clock you look facts in the face and admit that you are not tired (because you are not, you know), and that you arrange your evening so that it is not cut in the middle by a meal. By so doing you will have a clear expanse of at least three hours. I do not suggest that you should employ three hours every night of your life in using up your mental energy. But I do suggest that you might, for a commencement, employ an hour and a half every other evening in some important and consecutive cultivation of the mind. You will still be left with three evenings for friends, bridge, tennis, domestic scenes, odd reading, pipes, gardening, pottering, and prize competitions. You will still have the terrific wealth of forty-four hours between 2 P.M. Saturday and 10 A.M. Monday. If you persevere you will soon want to pass four evenings and perhaps five, in some sustained endeavour to be genuinely alive. And you will fall out of that habit of muttering to yourself at 11.15 P.M., "Time to be thinking about going to bed." The man who begins to go to bed forty minutes before he opens his bedroom door is bored; that is to say, he is not living.

But remember, at the start, those ninety nocturnal minutes thrice a week must be the most important minutes in the ten thousand and eighty. They must be sacred, quite as sacred as a dramatic rehearsal or a tennis match. Instead of saying, "Sorry I can't see you, old chap, but I have to run off to the tennis club," you must say, ". . . but I have to work." This, I admit, is intensely difficult to say. Tennis is so much more urgent than the immortal soul.

VI

Remember Human Nature

I have incidentally mentioned the vast expanse of forty-four hours between leaving business at 2 P.M. on Saturday and returning to business at 10 A.M. on Monday. And here I must touch on the point whether the week should consist of six days or of seven. For many years—in fact, until I was approaching forty—my own week consisted of seven days. I was constantly being informed by older and wiser people that more work, more genuine living, could be got out of six days than out of seven.

And it is certainly true that now, with one day in seven in which I follow no programme and make no effort save what the caprice of the moment dictates, I appreciate intensely the moral value of a weekly rest. Nevertheless, had I my life to arrange over again, I would do again as I have done. Only those who have lived at the full stretch seven days a week for a long time can appreciate the full beauty of a regular-recurring idleness. Moreover, I am ageing. And it is a question of age. In cases of abounding youth and exceptional energy and desire for effort I should say unhesitatingly: Keep going, day in, day out.

But in the average case I should say: Confine your formal programme (super-programme, I mean) to six days a week. If you find yourself wishing to extend it, extend it, but only in proportion to your wish; and count the time extra as a windfall, not as regular income, so that you can return to a six-day programme without the sensation of being poorer, of being a backslider.

Let us now see where we stand. So far we have marked for saving out of the waste of days, half an hour at least on six mornings a week, and one hour and a half on three evenings a week. Total, seven hours and a half a week.

I propose to be content with that seven hours and a half for the present. "What?" you cry. "You pretend to show us how to live, and you only deal with seven hours and a half out of a hundred and sixty-eight! Are you going to perform a miracle with your seven hours and a half?" Well, not to mince the matter, I am—if you will kindly let me! That is to say, I am going to ask you to attempt an experience which, while perfectly natural and explicable, has all the air of a miracle. My contention is that the full use of those seven-and-a-half hours will quicken the whole life of the week, add zest to it, and increase the interest which you feel in even the most banal occupations. You practise physical exercises for a mere ten minutes morning and evening, and yet you are not astonished when your physical health and strength are beneficially affected every hour of the day, and your whole physical outlook changed. Why should you be astonished that an average of over an hour a day given to the mind should permanently and completely enliven the whole activity of the mind?

More time might assuredly be given to the cultivation of one's self. And in proportion as the time was longer the results would be greater. But I prefer to begin with what looks like a trifling effort.

It is not really a trifling effort, as those will discover who have yet to essay it. To "clear" even seven hours and a half from the jungle is passably difficult. For some sacrifice has to be made. One may have spent one's time badly, but one did spend it; one did do something with it, however ill-advised that something may have been. To do something else means a change of habits.

And habits are the very dickens to change! Further, any change, even a change for the better, is always accompanied by drawbacks and discomforts. If you imagine that you will be able to devote seven hours and a half a week to serious, continuous effort, and still live your old life, you are mistaken. I repeat that some sacrifice, and an immense deal of volition, will be necessary. And it is because I know the difficulty, it is because I know the almost disastrous effect of failure in such an enterprise, that

I earnestly advise a very humble beginning. You must safeguard
your self-respect. Self-respect is at the root of all purposeful-
ness, and a failure in an enterprise deliberately planned deals a
desperate wound at one's self-respect. Hence I iterate and reit-
erate: Start quietly, unostentatiously.

When you have conscientiously given seven hours and a half
a week to the cultivation of your vitality for three months—then
you may begin to sing louder and tell yourself what wondrous
things you are capable of doing.

Before coming to the method of using the indicated hours, I
have one final suggestion to make. That is, as regards the
evenings, to allow much more than an hour and a half in which
to do the work of an hour and a half. Remember the chance of
accidents. Remember human nature. And give yourself, say,
from 9 to 11.30 for your task of ninety minutes.

VII

CONTROLLING THE MIND

People say: "One can't help one's thoughts." But one can. The control of the thinking machine is perfectly possible. And since nothing whatever happens to us outside our own brain; since nothing hurts us or gives us pleasure except within the brain, the supreme importance of being able to control what goes on in that mysterious brain is patent. This idea is one of the oldest platitudes, but it is a platitude whose profound truth and urgency most people live and die without realising. People complain of the lack of power to concentrate, not witting that they may acquire the power, if they choose.

And without the power to concentrate—that is to say, without the power to dictate to the brain its task and to ensure obedience—true life is impossible. Mind control is the first element of a full existence.

Hence, it seems to me, the first business of the day should be to put the mind through its paces. You look after your body, inside and out; you run grave danger in hacking hairs off your skin; you employ a whole army of individuals, from the milkman to the pig-killer, to enable you to bribe your stomach into decent behaviour. Why not devote a little attention to the far more delicate machinery of the mind, especially as you will require no extraneous aid? It is for this portion of the art and craft of living that I have reserved the time from the moment of quitting your door to the moment of arriving at your office.

"What? I am to cultivate my mind in the street, on the platform, in the train, and in the crowded street again?" Precisely.

Nothing simpler! No tools required! Not even a book. Nevertheless, the affair is not easy.

When you leave your house, concentrate your mind on a subject (no matter what, to begin with). You will not have gone ten yards before your mind has skipped away under your very eyes and is larking round the corner with another subject.

Bring it back by the scruff of the neck. Ere you have reached the station you will have brought it back about forty times. Do not despair. Continue. Keep it up. You will succeed. You cannot by any chance fail if you persevere. It is idle to pretend that your mind is incapable of concentration. Do you not remember that morning when you received a disquieting letter which demanded a very carefully-worded answer? How you kept your mind steadily on the subject of the answer, without a second's intermission, until you reached your office; whereupon you instantly sat down and wrote the answer? That was a case in which *you* were roused by circumstances to such a degree of vitality that you were able to dominate your mind like a tyrant. You would have no trifling. You insisted that its work should be done, and its work was done.

By the regular practice of concentration (as to which there is no secret—save the secret of perseverance) you can tyrannise over your mind (which is not the highest part of *you*) every hour of the day, and in no matter what place. The exercise is a very convenient one. If you got into your morning train with a pair of dumb-bells for your muscles or an encyclopædia in ten volumes for your learning, you would probably excite remark. But as you walk in the street, or sit in the corner of the compartment behind a pipe, or "strap-hang" on the Subterranean, who is to know that you are engaged in the most important of daily acts? What asinine boor can laugh at you?

I do not care what you concentrate on, so long as you concentrate. It is the mere disciplining of the thinking machine that counts. But still, you may as well kill two birds with one stone, and concentrate on something useful. I suggest—it is only a suggestion—a little chapter of Marcus Aurelius or Epictetus.

Do not, I beg, shy at their names. For myself, I know nothing more "actual," more bursting with plain common-sense, applicable to the daily life of plain persons like you and me (who hate airs, pose, and nonsense) than Marcus Aurelius or Epictetus. Read a chapter—and so short they are, the chapters!—in the evening and concentrate on it the next morning. You will see.

Yes, my friend, it is useless for you to try to disguise the fact. I can hear your brain like a telephone at my ear. You are saying to yourself: "This fellow was doing pretty well up to his seventh chapter. He had begun to interest me faintly. But what he says about thinking in trains, and concentration, and so on, is not for me. It may be well enough for some folks, but it isn't in my line."

It is for you, I passionately repeat; it is for you. Indeed, you are the very man I am aiming at.

Throw away the suggestion, and you throw away the most precious suggestion that was ever offered to you. It is not my suggestion. It is the suggestion of the most sensible, practical, hard-headed men that have walked the earth. I only give it you at second-hand. Try it. Get your mind in hand. And see how the process cures half the evils of life—especially worry, that miserable, avoidable, shameful disease—worry!

VIII

THE REFLECTIVE MOOD

The exercise of concentrating the mind (to which at least half an hour a day should be given) is a mere preliminary, like scales on the piano. Having acquired power over that most unruly member of one's complex organism, one has naturally to put it to the yoke. Useless to possess an obedient mind unless one profits to the furthest possible degree by its obedience. A prolonged primary course of study is indicated.

Now as to what this course of study should be there cannot be any question; there never has been any question. All the sensible people of all ages are agreed upon it. And it is not literature, nor is it any other art, nor is it history, nor is it any science. It is the study of one's self. Man, know thyself. These words are so hackneyed that verily I blush to write them. Yet they must be written, for they need to be written. (I take back my blush, being ashamed of it.) Man, know thyself. I say it out loud. The phrase is one of those phrases with which everyone is familiar, of which everyone acknowledges the value, and which only the most sagacious put into practice. I don't know why. I am entirely convinced that what is more than anything else lacking in the life of the average well-intentioned man of to-day is the reflective mood.

We do not reflect. I mean that we do not reflect upon genuinely important things; upon the problem of our happiness, upon the main direction in which we are going, upon what life is giving to us, upon the share which reason has (or has not) in determining our actions, and upon the relation between our principles and our conduct.

And yet you are in search of happiness, are you not? Have you discovered it?

The chances are that you have not. The chances are that you have already come to believe that happiness is unattainable. But men have attained it. And they have attained it by realising that happiness does not spring from the procuring of physical or mental pleasure, but from the development of reason and the adjustment of conduct to principles.

I suppose that you will not have the audacity to deny this. And if you admit it, and still devote no part of your day to the deliberate consideration of your reason, principles, and conduct, you admit also that while striving for a certain thing you are regularly leaving undone the one act which is necessary to the attainment of that thing.

Now, shall I blush, or will you?

Do not fear that I mean to thrust certain principles upon your attention. I care not (in this place) what your principles are. Your principles may induce you to believe in the righteousness of burglary. I don't mind. All I urge is that a life in which conduct does not fairly well accord with principles is a silly life; and that conduct can only be made to accord with principles by means of daily examination, reflection, and resolution. What leads to the permanent sorrowfulness of burglars is that their principles are contrary to burglary. If they genuinely believed in the moral excellence of burglary, penal servitude would simply mean so many happy years for them; all martyrs are happy, because their conduct and their principles agree.

As for reason (which makes conduct, and is not unconnected with the making of principles), it plays a far smaller part in our lives than we fancy. We are supposed to be reasonable, but we are much more instinctive than reasonable. And the less we reflect, the less reasonable we shall be. The next time you get cross with the waiter because your steak is over-cooked, ask reason to step into the cabinet-room of your mind, and consult her. She will probably tell you that the waiter did not cook the steak, and had no control over the cooking of the steak; and that even if he alone was to blame, you accomplished nothing good by getting cross; you merely lost your dignity, looked a fool in the eyes of sensible men, and soured the waiter, while producing no effect whatever on the steak.

The result of this consultation with reason (for which she makes no charge) will be that when once more your steak is over-cooked you will treat the waiter as a fellow-creature, remain quite calm in a kindly spirit, and politely insist on having a fresh steak. The gain will be obvious and solid.

In the formation or modification of principles, and the practice of conduct, much help can be derived from printed books (issued at sixpence each and upwards). I mentioned in my last chapter Marcus Aurelius and Epictetus. Certain even more widely known works will occur at once to the memory. I may also mention Pascal, La Bruyère, and Emerson. For myself, you do not catch me travelling without my Marcus Aurelius. Yes, books are valuable. But no reading of books will take the place of a daily, candid, honest examination of what one has recently done, and what one is about to do—of a steady looking at one's self in the face (disconcerting though the sight may be).

When shall this important business be accomplished? The solitude of the evening journey home appears to me to be suitable for it. A reflective mood naturally follows the exertion of having earned the day's living. Of course if, instead of attending to an elementary and profoundly important duty, you prefer to read the paper (which you might just as well read while waiting for your dinner) I have nothing to say. But attend to it at some time of the day you must. I now come to the evening hours.

IX

INTEREST IN THE ARTS

Many people pursue a regular and uninterrupted course of idleness in the evenings because they think that there is no alternative to idleness but the study of literature; and they do not happen to have a taste for literature. This is a great mistake.

Of course it is impossible, or at any rate very difficult, properly to study anything whatever without the aid of printed books. But if you desired to understand the deeper depths of bridge or of boat-sailing you would not be deterred by your lack of interest in literature from reading the best books on bridge or boat-sailing. We must, therefore, distinguish between literature, and books treating of subjects not literary. I shall come to literature in due course.

Let me now remark to those who have never read Meredith, and who are capable of being unmoved by a discussion as to whether Mr. Stephen Phillips is or is not a true poet, that they are perfectly within their rights. It is not a crime not to love literature. It is not a sign of imbecility. The mandarins of literature will order out to instant execution the unfortunate individual who does not comprehend, say, the influence of Wordsworth on Tennyson. But that is only their impudence. Where would they be, I wonder, if requested to explain the influences that went to make Tschaikowsky's "Pathetic Symphony"?

There are enormous fields of knowledge quite outside literature which will yield magnificent results to cultivators. For example (since I have just mentioned the most popular piece of high-class music in England to-day), I am reminded that the

Promenade Concerts begin in August. You go to them. You smoke your cigar or cigarette (and I regret to say that you strike your matches during the soft bars of the "Lohengrin" overture), and you enjoy the music. But you say you cannot play the piano or the fiddle, or even the banjo; that you know nothing of music.

What does that matter? That you have a genuine taste for music is proved by the fact that, in order to fill his hall with you and your peers, the conductor is obliged to provide programmes from which bad music is almost entirely excluded (a change from the old Covent Garden days!).

Now surely your inability to perform "The Maiden's Prayer" on a piano need not prevent you from making yourself familiar with the construction of the orchestra to which you listen a couple of nights a week during a couple of months! As things are, you probably think of the orchestra as a heterogeneous mass of instruments producing a confused agreeable mass of sound. You do not listen for details because you have never trained your ears to listen to details.

If you were asked to name the instruments which play the great theme at the beginning of the C minor symphony you could not name them for your life's sake. Yet you admire the C minor symphony. It has thrilled you. It will thrill you again. You have even talked about it, in an expansive mood, to that lady— you know whom I mean. And all you can positively state about the C minor symphony is that Beethoven composed it and that it is a "jolly fine thing."

Now, if you have read, say, Mr. Krehbiel's "How to Listen to Music" (which can be got at any bookseller's for less than the price of a stall at the Alhambra, and which contains photographs of all the orchestral instruments and plans of the arrangement of orchestras) you would next go to a promenade concert with an astonishing intensification of interest in it. Instead of a confused mass, the orchestra would appear to you as what it is—a marvellously balanced organism whose various groups of members each have a different and an indispensable function. You would spy out the instruments, and listen for their respective sounds. You would know the gulf that separates a French horn from an English horn, and you would perceive why a player of the hautboy gets higher wages than a fiddler, though the fiddle is the more difficult instrument. You would *live* at a promenade concert, whereas previously you had merely existed there in a state of beatific coma, like a baby gazing at a bright object.

The foundations of a genuine, systematic knowledge of music might be laid. You might specialise your inquiries either on a particular form of music (such as the symphony), or on the works of a particular composer. At the end of a year of forty-eight weeks of three brief evenings each, combined with a study of programmes and attendances at concerts chosen out of your increasing knowledge, you would really know something about music, even though you were as far off as ever from jangling "The Maiden's Prayer" on the piano.

"But I hate music!" you say. My dear sir, I respect you.

What applies to music applies to the other arts. I might mention Mr. Clermont Witt's "How to Look at Pictures," or Mr. Russell Sturgis's "How to Judge Architecture," as beginnings (merely beginnings) of systematic vitalising knowledge in other arts, the materials for whose study abound in London.

"I hate all the arts!" you say. My dear sir, I respect you more and more.

I will deal with your case next, before coming to literature.

X

Nothing in Life Is Humdrum

Art is a great thing. But it is not the greatest. The most important of all perceptions is the continual perception of cause
and effect—in other words, the perception of the continuous
development of the universe—in still other words, the perception of the course of evolution. When one has thoroughly got
imbued into one's head the leading truth that nothing happens
without a cause, one grows not only large-minded, but large-
hearted.

It is hard to have one's watch stolen, but one reflects that the
thief of the watch became a thief from causes of heredity and
environment which are as interesting as they are scientifically
comprehensible; and one buys another watch, if not with joy, at
any rate with a philosophy that makes bitterness impossible.
One loses, in the study of cause and effect, that absurd air which
so many people have of being always shocked and pained by the
curiousness of life. Such people live amid human nature as if
human nature were a foreign country full of awful foreign customs. But, having reached maturity, one ought surely to be
ashamed of being a stranger in a strange land!

The study of cause and effect, while it lessens the painfulness
of life, adds to life's picturesqueness. The man to whom evolution is but a name looks at the sea as a grandiose, monotonous
spectacle, which he can witness in August for three shillings
third-class return. The man who is imbued with the idea of
development, of continuous cause and effect, perceives in the
sea an element which in the day-before-yesterday of geology

45

was vapour, which yesterday was boiling, and which to-morrow will inevitably be ice.

He perceives that a liquid is merely something on its way to be solid, and he is penetrated by a sense of the tremendous, changeful picturesqueness of life. Nothing will afford a more durable satisfaction than the constantly cultivated appreciation of this. It is the end of all science.

Cause and effect are to be found everywhere. Rents went up in Shepherd's Bush. It was painful and shocking that rents should go up in Shepherd's Bush. But to a certain point we are all scientific students of cause and effect, and there was not a clerk lunching at a Lyons Restaurant who did not scientifically put two and two together and see in the (once) Two-penny Tube the cause of an excessive demand for wigwams in Shepherd's Bush, and in the excessive demand for wigwams the cause of the increase in the price of wigwams.

"Simple!" you say, disdainfully. Everything—the whole complex movement of the universe—is as simple as that—when you can sufficiently put two and two together. And, my dear sir, perhaps you happen to be an estate agent's clerk, and you hate the arts, and you want to foster your immortal soul, and you can't be interested in your business because it's so humdrum.

Nothing is humdrum.

The tremendous, changeful picturesqueness of life is marvellously shown in an estate agent's office. What! There was a block of traffic in Oxford Street; to avoid the block people actually began to travel under the cellars and drains, and the result was a rise of rents in Shepherd's Bush! And you say that isn't picturesque! Suppose you were to study, in this spirit, the property question in London for an hour and a half every other evening. Would it not give zest to your business, and transform your whole life?

You would arrive at more difficult problems. And you would be able to tell us why, as the natural result of cause and effect, the longest straight street in London is about a yard and a half in length, while the longest absolutely straight street in Paris extends for miles. I think you will admit that in an estate agent's clerk I have not chosen an example that specially favours my theories.

You are a bank clerk, and you have not read that breathless romance (disguised as a scientific study), Walter Bagehot's "Lombard Street"? Ah, my dear sir, if you had begun with that, and followed it up for ninety minutes every other evening, how enthralling your business would be to you, and how much more clearly you would understand human nature.

You are "penned in town," but you love excursions to the country and the observation of wild life—certainly a heart-enlarging diversion. Why don't you walk out of your house door, in your slippers, to the nearest gas lamp of a night with a butterfly net, and observe the wild life of common and rare moths that is beating about it, and co-ordinate the knowledge thus obtained and build a superstructure on it, and at last get to *know* something about something?

You need not be devoted to the arts, nor to literature, in order to live fully.

The whole field of daily habit and scene is waiting to satisfy that curiosity which means life, and the satisfaction of which means an understanding heart.

I promised to deal with your case, O man who hates art and literature, and I have dealt with it. I now come to the case of the person, happily very common, who *does* "like reading."

XI

SERIOUS READING

Novels are excluded from "serious reading," so that the man who, bent on self-improvement, has been deciding to devote ninety minutes three times a week to a complete study of the works of Charles Dickens will be well advised to alter his plans. The reason is not that novels are not serious—some of the great literature of the world is in the form of prose fiction—the reason is that bad novels ought not to be read, and that good novels never demand any appreciable mental application on the part of the reader. It is only the bad parts of Meredith's novels that are difficult. A good novel rushes you forward like a skiff down a stream, and you arrive at the end, perhaps breathless, but unexhausted. The best novels involve the least strain. Now in the cultivation of the mind one of the most important factors is precisely the feeling of strain, of difficulty, of a task which one part of you is anxious to achieve and another part of you is anxious to shirk; and that feeling cannot be got in facing a novel. You do not set your teeth in order to read "Anna Karenina." Therefore, though you should read novels, you should not read them in those ninety minutes.

Imaginative poetry produces a far greater mental strain than novels. It produces probably the severest strain of any form of literature. It is the highest form of literature. It yields the highest form of pleasure, and teaches the highest form of wisdom. In a word, there is nothing to compare with it. I say this with sad consciousness of the fact that the majority of people do not read poetry.

I am persuaded that many excellent persons, if they were confronted with the alternatives of reading "Paradise Lost" and
going round Trafalgar Square at noonday on their knees in sack-
cloth, would choose the ordeal of public ridicule. Still, I will
never cease advising my friends and enemies to read poetry
before anything.

If poetry is what is called "a sealed book" to you, begin by
reading Hazlitt's famous essay on the nature of "poetry in general." It is the best thing of its kind in English, and no one who
has read it can possibly be under the misapprehension that
poetry is a mediæval torture, or a mad elephant, or a gun that
will go off by itself and kill at forty paces. Indeed, it is difficult
to imagine the mental state of the man who, after reading
Hazlitt's essay, is not urgently desirous of reading some poetry
before his next meal. If the essay so inspires you I would suggest
that you make a commencement with purely narrative poetry.

There is an infinitely finer English novel, written by a woman,
than anything by George Eliot or the Brontës, or even Jane
Austen, which perhaps you have not read. Its title is "Aurora
Leigh," and its author E. B. Browning. It happens to be written
in verse, and to contain a considerable amount of genuinely fine
poetry. Decide to read that book through, even if you die for it.
Forget that it is fine poetry. Read it simply for the story and the
social ideas. And when you have done, ask yourself honestly
whether you still dislike poetry. I have known more than one
person to whom "Aurora Leigh" has been the means of proving
that in assuming they hated poetry they were entirely mistaken.

Of course, if, after Hazlitt, and such an experiment made in
the light of Hazlitt, you are finally assured that there is something in you which is antagonistic to poetry, you must be content
with history or philosophy. I shall regret it, yet not inconsolably.
"The Decline and Fall" is not to be named in the same day with
"Paradise Lost," but it is a vastly pretty thing; and Herbert
Spencer's "First Principles" simply laughs at the claims of
poetry, and refuses to be accepted as aught but the most majestic product of any human mind. I do not suggest that either of
these works is suitable for a tyro in mental strains. But I see no
reason why any man of average intelligence should not, after a

year of continuous reading, be fit to assault the supreme masterpieces of history or philosophy. The great convenience of
masterpieces is that they are so astonishingly lucid.

I suggest no particular work as a start. The attempt would be
futile in the space at my command. But I have two general suggestions of a certain importance. The first is to define the direction and scope of your efforts. Choose a limited period, or a
limited subject, or a single author. Say to yourself: "I will know
something about the French Revolution, or the rise of railways,
or the works of John Keats." And during a given period, to be
settled beforehand, confine yourself to your choice. There is
much pleasure to be derived from being a specialist.

The second suggestion is to think as well as to read. I know
people who read and read, and for all the good it does them they
might just as well cut bread-and-butter. They take to reading as
better men take to drink. They fly through the shires of literature on a motor-car, their sole object being motion. They will tell
you how many books they have read in a year.

Unless you give at least forty-five minutes to careful, fatiguing
reflection (it is an awful bore at first) upon what you are reading, your ninety minutes of a night are chiefly wasted. This
means that your pace will be slow.

Never mind.

Forget the goal; think only of the surrounding country; and
after a period, perhaps when you least expect it, you will suddenly find yourself in a lovely town on a hill.

XII

Dangers to Avoid

I cannot terminate these hints, often, I fear, too didactic and abrupt, upon the full use of one's time to the great end of living (as distinguished from vegetating) without briefly referring to certain dangers which lie in wait for the sincere aspirant towards life. The first is the terrible danger of becoming that most odious and least supportable of persons—a prig. Now a prig is a pert fellow who gives himself airs of superior wisdom. A prig is a pompous fool who has gone out for a ceremonial walk, and without knowing it has lost an important part of his attire, namely, his sense of humour. A prig is a tedious individual who, having made a discovery, is so impressed by his discovery that he is capable of being gravely displeased because the entire world is not also impressed by it. Unconsciously to become a prig is an easy and a fatal thing.

Hence, when one sets forth on the enterprise of using all one's time, it is just as well to remember that one's own time, and not other people's time, is the material with which one has to deal; that the earth rolled on pretty comfortably before one began to balance a budget of the hours, and that it will continue to roll on pretty comfortably whether or not one succeeds in one's new role of chancellor of the exchequer of time. It is as well not to chatter too much about what one is doing, and not to betray a too-pained sadness at the spectacle of a whole world deliberately wasting so many hours out of every day, and therefore never really living. It will be found, ultimately, that in taking care of one's self one has quite all one can do.

Another danger is the danger of being tied to a programme like a slave to a chariot. One's programme must not be allowed to run away with one. It must be respected, but it must not be worshipped as a fetish. A programme of daily employ is not a religion.

This seems obvious. Yet I know men whose lives are a burden to themselves and a distressing burden to their relatives and friends simply because they have failed to appreciate the obvious. "Oh, no," I have heard the martyred wife exclaim, "Arthur always takes the dog out for exercise at eight o'clock and he always begins to read at a quarter to nine. So it's quite out of the question that we should . . ." etc., etc. And the note of absolute finality in that plaintive voice reveals the unsuspected and ridiculous tragedy of a career.

On the other hand, a programme is a programme. And unless it is treated with deference it ceases to be anything but a poor joke. To treat one's programme with exactly the right amount of deference, to live with not too much and not too little elasticity, is scarcely the simple affair it may appear to the inexperienced.

And still another danger is the danger of developing a policy of rush, of being gradually more and more obsessed by what one has to do next. In this way one may come to exist as in a prison, and one's life may cease to be one's own. One may take the dog out for a walk at eight o'clock, and meditate the whole time on the fact that one must begin to read at a quarter to nine, and that one must not be late.

And the occasional deliberate breaking of one's programme will not help to mend matters. The evil springs not from persisting without elasticity in what one has attempted, but from originally attempting too much, from filling one's programme till it runs over. The only cure is to reconstitute the programme, and to attempt less.

But the appetite for knowledge grows by what it feeds on, and there are men who come to like a constant breathless hurry of endeavour. Of them it may be said that a constant breathless hurry is better than an eternal doze.

In any case, if the programme exhibits a tendency to be oppressive, and yet one wishes not to modify it, an excellent palliative is to pass with exaggerated deliberation from one portion of it to another; for example, to spend five minutes in perfect mental quiescence between chaining up the St. Bernard and opening the book; in other words, to waste five minutes with the entire consciousness of wasting them.

The last, and chiefest danger which I would indicate, is one to which I have already referred—the risk of a failure at the commencement of the enterprise.

I must insist on it.

A failure at the commencement may easily kill outright the newborn impulse towards a complete vitality, and therefore every precaution should be observed to avoid it. The impulse must not be over-taxed. Let the pace of the first lap be even absurdly slow, but let it be as regular as possible.

And, having once decided to achieve a certain task, achieve it at all costs of tedium and distaste. The gain in self-confidence of having accomplished a tiresome labour is immense.

Finally, in choosing the first occupations of those evening hours, be guided by nothing whatever but your taste and natural inclination.

It is a fine thing to be a walking encyclopædia of philosophy, but if you happen to have no liking for philosophy, and to have a liking for the natural history of street-cries, much better leave philosophy alone, and take to street-cries.

The Human Machine.

Contents

I

TAKING ONESELF FOR GRANTED

There are men who are capable of loving a machine more deeply than they can love a woman. They are among the happiest men on earth. This is not a sneer meanly shot from cover at women. It is simply a statement of notorious fact. Men who worry themselves to distraction over the perfecting of a machine are indubitably blessed beyond their kind. Most of us have known such men. Yesterday they were constructing motor-cars. But to-day aeroplanes are in the air—or, at any rate, they ought to be, according to the inventors. Watch the inventors. Invention is not usually their principal business. They must invent in their spare time. They must invent before breakfast, invent in the Strand between Lyons's and the office, invent after dinner, invent on Sundays. See with what ardour they rush home of a night! See how they seize a half-holiday, like hungry dogs a bone! They don't want golf, bridge, limericks, novels, illustrated magazines, clubs, whisky, starting-prices, hints about neckties, political meetings, yarns, comic songs, anturic salts, nor the smiles that are situate between a gay corsage and a picture hat. They never wonder, at a loss, what they will do next. Their evenings never drag—are always too short. You may, indeed, catch them at twelve o'clock at night on the flat of their backs; but not in bed! No, in a shed, under the machine, holding a candle (whose paths drop fatness) up to the connecting-rod that is strained, or the wheel that is out of centre. They are continually interested, nay, enthralled. They have a machine, and they are perfecting it. They get one part right, and then another goes wrong; and they get that right, and then another goes wrong, and so on. When they are quite sure they have reached perfection, forth issues the machine out of the shed— and in five minutes is smashed up, together with a limb or so of the inventors, just because they had been quite sure too soon. Then the whole business starts again. They do not give up—that particular wreck was, of course, due to a mere oversight; the whole business starts again. For they have glimpsed perfection; they have the gleam of perfection in their souls. Thus their lives run away. "They will never fly!" you remark, cynically. Well, if they don't? Besides, what about Wright? With all your cynicism, have you never envied them their machine and their passionate interest in it?

You know, perhaps, the moment when, brushing in front of the glass, you detected your first grey hair. You stopped brushing; then you resumed brushing, hastily; you pretended not to be shocked, but you were. Perhaps you know a more disturbing moment than that, the moment when it suddenly occurred to you that you had "arrived" as far as you ever will arrive; and you had realised as much of your early dream as you ever will realise, and the realisation was utterly unlike the dream; and marriage was excessively prosaic and eternal, not at all what you expected it to be; and your illusions were dissipated; and games and hobbies had an unpleasant core of tedium and futility; and the ideal tobacco-mixture did not exist; and one literary masterpiece resembled another; and all the days that are to come will more or less resemble the present day, until you die; and in an illuminating flash you understood what all those people were driving at when they wrote such unconscionably long letters to the *Telegraph* as to life being worth living or not worth living; and there was naught to be done but face the grey, monotonous future, and pretend to be cheerful with the worm of *ennui* gnawing at your heart! In a word, the moment when it occurred to you that yours is "the common lot." In that moment have you not wished—do you not continually wish—for an exhaustless machine, a machine that you could never get to the end of? Would you not give your head to be lying on the flat of your back, peering with a candle, dirty, foiled, catching cold—but absorbed in the pursuit of an object? Have you not gloomily regretted that you were born without a mechanical turn, because there is really something about a machine . . . ?

It has never struck you that you do possess a machine! Oh, blind! Oh, dull! It has never struck you that you have at hand a machine wonderful beyond all mechanisms in sheds, intricate, delicately adjustable, of astounding and miraculous possibilities, interminably interesting! That machine is yourself. "This fellow is preaching. I won't have it!" you exclaim resentfully. Dear sir, I am not preaching, and, even if I were, I think you *would* have it. I think I can anyhow keep hold of your button for a while, though you pull hard. I am not preaching. I am simply bent on calling your attention to a fact which has perhaps wholly or partially escaped you—namely, that you are the most fascinating bit of machinery that ever was. You do yourself less than justice. It is said that men are only interested in themselves. The truth is that, as a rule, men are interested in every mortal thing except themselves. They have a habit of taking themselves for granted, and that habit is responsible for nine-tenths of the boredom and despair on the face of the planet.

A man will wake up in the middle of the night (usually owing to some form of delightful excess), and his brain will be very active indeed for a space ere he can go to sleep again. In that candid hour, after the exaltation of the evening and before the hope of the dawn, he will see everything in its true colours— except himself. There is nothing like a sleepless couch for a clear vision of one's environment. He will see all his wife's faults and the hopelessness of trying to cure them. He will momentarily see, though with less sharpness of outline, his own faults. He will probably decide that the anxieties of children outweigh the joys connected with children. He will admit all the short-comings of existence, will face them like a man, grimly, sourly, in a sturdy despair. He will mutter: "Of course I'm angry! Who wouldn't be? Of course I'm disappointed! Did I expect this twenty years ago? Yes, we ought to save more. But we don't, so there you are! I'm bound to worry! I know I should be better if I didn't smoke so much. I know there's absolutely no sense at all in taking liqueurs. Absurd to be ruffled with her when she's in one of her moods. I don't have enough exercise. Can't be regular, somehow. Not the slightest use hoping that things will be different, because I know they won't. Queer world! Never really what you may call happy, you know. Now, if things were different . . ." He loses consciousness.

Observe: he has taken himself for granted, just glancing at his faults and looking away again. It is his environment that has occupied his attention, and his environment—"things"—that he would wish to have "different," did he not know, out of the fulness of experience, that it is futile to desire such a change? What he wants is a pipe that won't put itself into his mouth, a glass that won't leap of its own accord to his lips, money that won't slip untouched out of his pocket, legs that without asking will carry him certain miles every day in the open air, habits that practise themselves, a wife that will expand and contract according to his humours, like a Wernicke bookcase, always complete but never finished. Wise man, he perceives at once that he can't have these things. And so he resigns himself to the universe, and settles down to a permanent, restrained discontent. No one shall say he is unreasonable.

You see, he has given no attention to the machine. Let us not call it a flying-machine. Let us call it simply an automobile. There it is on the road, jolting, screeching, rattling, perfuming. And there he is, saying: "This road ought to be as smooth as velvet. That hill in front is ridiculous, and the descent on the other side positively dangerous. And it's all turns—I can't see a hundred yards in front." He has a wild idea of trying to force the County Council to sand-paper the road, or of employing the new Territorial Army to remove the hill. But he dismisses that idea—he is so reasonable. He accepts all. He sits clothed in reasonableness on the machine, and accepts all. "Ass!" you exclaim. "Why doesn't he get down and inflate that tyre, for one thing? Anyone can see the sparkling apparatus is wrong, and it's perfectly certain the gear-box wants oil. Why doesn't he——?" I will tell you why he doesn't. Just because he isn't aware that he is on a machine at all. He has never examined what he is on. And at the back of his consciousness is a dim idea that he is perched on a piece of solid, immutable rock that runs on castors.

II

AMATEURS IN THE ART OF LIVING

Considering that we have to spend the whole of our lives in this human machine, considering that it is our sole means of contact and compromise with the rest of the world, we really do devote to it very little attention. When I say "we," I mean our inmost spirits, the instinctive part, the mystery within that exists. And when I say "the human machine" I mean the brain and the body—and chiefly the brain. The expression of the soul by means of the brain and body is what we call the art of "living." We certainly do not learn this art at school to any appreciable extent. At school we are taught that it is necessary to fling our arms and legs to and fro for so many hours per diem. We are also shown, practically, that our brains are capable of performing certain useful tricks, and that if we do not compel our brains to perform those tricks we shall suffer. Thus one day we run home and proclaim to our delighted parents that eleven twelves are 132. A feat of the brain! So it goes on until our parents begin to look up to us because we can chatter of cosines or sketch the foreign policy of Louis XIV. Good! But not a word about the principles of the art of living yet! Only a few detached rules from our parents, to be blindly followed when particular crises supervene. And, indeed, it would be absurd to talk to a schoolboy about the expression of his soul. He would probably mutter a monosyllable which is not "mice."

Of course, school is merely a preparation for living; unless one goes to a university, in which case it is a preparation for university. One is supposed to turn one's attention to living when these preliminaries are over—say at the age of about twenty. Assuredly one lives then; there is, however, nothing new in that, for one has been living all the time, in a fashion; all the time one has been using the machine without understanding it. But does one, school and college being over, enter upon a study of the machine? Not a bit. The question then becomes, not how to live, but how to obtain and retain a position in which one will be able to live; how to get minute portions of dead animals and plants which one can swallow, in order not to die of hunger; how to acquire and constantly renew a stock of other portions of dead animals and plants in which one can envelop oneself in order not to die of cold; how to procure the exclusive right of entry into certain huts where one may sleep and eat without being rained upon by the clouds of heaven. And so forth. And when one has realised this ambition, there comes the desire to be able to double the operation and do it, not for oneself alone, but for oneself and another. Marriage! But no scientific sustained attention is yet given to the real business of living, of smooth intercourse, of self-expression, of conscious adaptation to environment—in brief, to the study of the machine. At thirty the chances are that a man will understand better the draught of a chimney than his own respiratory apparatus—to name one of the simple, obvious things—and as for understanding the working of his own brain—what an idea! As for the skill to avoid the waste of power involved by friction in the business of living, do we give an hour to it in a month? Do we ever at all examine it save in an amateurish and clumsy fashion? A young lady produces a water-colour drawing. "Very nice!" we say, and add, to ourselves, "For an amateur." But our living is more amateurish than that young lady's drawing; though surely we ought every one of us to be professionals at living!

When we have been engaged in the preliminaries to living for about fifty-five years, we begin to think about slacking off. Up till this period our reason for not having scientifically studied the art of living—the perfecting and use of the finer parts of the machine—is not that we have lacked leisure (most of us have enormous heaps of leisure), but that we have simply been too absorbed in the preliminaries, have, in fact, treated the preliminaries to the business as the business itself. Then at fifty-five we ought at last to begin to live our lives with professional skill, as a professional painter paints pictures. Yes, but we can't. It is too late then. Neither painters, nor acrobats, nor any professionals can be formed at the age of fifty-five. Thus we finish our lives amateurishly, as we have begun them. And when the machine creaks and sets our teeth on edge, or refuses to obey the steering-wheel and deposits us in the ditch, we say: "Can't be helped!" or "Doesn't matter! It will be all the same a hundred years hence!" or: "I must make the best of things." And we try to believe that in accepting the *status quo* we have justified the *status quo*, and all the time we feel our insincerity.

You exclaim that I exaggerate. I do. To force into prominence an aspect of affairs usually overlooked, it is absolutely necessary to exaggerate. Poetic license is one name for this kind of exaggeration. But I exaggerate very little indeed, much less than perhaps you think. I know that you are going to point out to me that vast numbers of people regularly spend a considerable portion of their leisure in striving after self-improvement. Granted! And I am glad of it. But I should be gladder if their strivings bore more closely upon the daily business of living, of self-expression without friction and without futile desires. See this man who regularly studies every evening of his life! He has genuinely understood the nature of poetry, and his taste is admirable. He recites verse with true feeling, and may be said to be highly cultivated. Poetry is a continual source of pleasure to him. True! But why is he always complaining about not receiving his deserts in the office? Why is he worried about finance? Why does he so often sulk with his wife? Why does he persist in eating more than his digestion will tolerate? It was not written in the book of fate that he should complain and worry and sulk and suffer. And if he was a professional at living he would not do these things. There is no reason why he should do them, except the reason that he has never learnt his business, never studied the human machine as a whole, never really thought rationally about living. Supposing you encountered an automobilist who was swerving and grinding all over the road, and you stopped to ask what was the matter, and he replied: "Never mind what's the matter. Just look at my lovely acetylene lamps, how they shine, and how I've polished them!" You would not regard him as a Clifford-Earp, or even as an entirely sane man. So with our student of poetry. It is indubitable that a large amount of what is known as self-improvement is simply self-indulgence—a form of pleasure which only incidentally improves a particular part of the machine, and even that to the neglect of far more important parts.

My aim is to direct a man's attention to himself as a whole, considered as a machine, complex and capable of quite extraordinary efficiency, for travelling through this world smoothly, in any desired manner, with satisfaction not only to himself but to the people he meets *en route*, and the people who are overtaking him and whom he is overtaking. My aim is to show that only an inappreciable fraction of our ordered and sustained efforts is given to the business of actual living, as distinguished from the preliminaries to living.

III

The Brain as a Gentleman-at-Large

It is not as if, in this business of daily living, we were seriously hampered by ignorance either as to the results which we ought to obtain, or as to the general means which we must employ in order to obtain them. With all our absorption in the mere preliminaries to living, and all our carelessness about living itself, we arrive pretty soon at a fairly accurate notion of what satisfactory living is, and we perceive with some clearness the methods necessary to success. I have pictured the man who wakes up in the middle of the night and sees the horrid semi-fiasco of his life. But let me picture the man who wakes up refreshed early on a fine summer morning and looks into his mind with the eyes of hope and experience, not experience and despair. That man will pass a delightful half-hour in thinking upon the scheme of the universe as it affects himself. He is quite clear that contentment depends on his own acts, and that no power can prevent him from performing those acts. He plans everything out, and before he gets up he knows precisely what he must and will do in certain foreseen crises and junctures. He sincerely desires to live efficiently—who would wish to make a daily mess of existence?—and he knows the way to realise the desire.

And yet, mark me! That man will not have been an hour on his feet on this difficult earth before the machine has unmistakably gone wrong: the machine which was designed to do this work of living, which is capable of doing it thoroughly well, but which has not been put into order! What is the use of consulting the map of life and tracing the itinerary, and getting the machine out of the shed, and making a start, if half the nuts are loose, or the steering pillar is twisted, or there is no petrol in the tank? (Having asked this question, I will drop the mechanico-vehicular comparison, which is too rough and crude for the delicacy of the subject.) Where has the human machine gone wrong? It has gone wrong in the brain. What, is he "wrong in the head"? Most assuredly, most strictly. He knows—none better—that when his wife employs a particular tone containing ten grains of asperity, and he replies in a particular tone containing eleven grains, the consequences will be explosive. He knows, on the other hand, that if he replies in a tone containing only one little drop of honey, the consequences may not be unworthy of two reasonable beings. He knows this. His brain is fully instructed. And lo! his brain, while arguing that women are really too absurd (as if that was the point), is sending down orders to the muscles of the throat and mouth which result in at least eleven grains of asperity, and conjugal relations are endangered for the day. He didn't want to do it. His desire was not to do it. He despises himself for doing it. But his brain was not in working order. His brain ran away—"raced"—on its own account, against reason, against desire, against morning resolves—and there he is!

That is just one example, of the simplest and slightest. Examples can be multiplied. The man may be a young man whose immediate future depends on his passing an examination—an examination which he is capable of passing "on his head," which nothing can prevent him from passing if only his brain will not be so absurd as to give orders to his legs to walk out of the house towards the tennis court instead of sending them upstairs to the study; if only, having once safely lodged him in the study, his brain will devote itself to the pages of books instead of dwelling on the image of a nice girl—not at all like other girls. Or the man may be an old man who will live in perfect comfort if only his brain will not interminably run round and round in a circle of grievances, apprehensions, and fears which no amount of contemplation can destroy or even ameliorate.

The brain, the brain—that is the seat of trouble! "Well," you say, "of course it is. We all know that!" We don't act as if we did, anyway. "Give us more brains, Lord!" ejaculated a great writer. Personally, I think he would have been wiser if he had asked first for the power to keep in order such brains as we have. We indubitably possess quite enough brains, quite as much as we can handle. The supreme muddlers of living are often people of quite remarkable intellectual faculty, with a quite remarkable gift of being wise for others. The pity is that our brains have a way of "wandering," as it is politely called. Brain-wandering is indeed now recognised as a specific disease. I wonder what you, O business man with an office in Ludgate Circus, would say to your office-boy, whom you had dispatched on an urgent message to Westminster, and whom you found larking around Euston Station when you rushed to catch your week-end train. "Please, sir, I started to go to Westminster, but there's something funny in my limbs that makes me go up all manner of streets. I can't help it, sir!" "Can't you?" you would say. "Well, you had better go and be somebody else's office-boy." Your brain is something worse than that office-boy, something more insidiously potent for evil.

I conceive the brain of the average well-intentioned man as possessing the tricks and manners of one of those gentlemen-at-large who, having nothing very urgent to do, stroll along and offer their services gratis to some shorthanded work of philanthropy. They will commonly demoralise and disorganise the business conduct of an affair in about a fortnight. They come when they like; they go when they like. Sometimes they are exceedingly industrious and obedient, but then there is an even chance that they will shirk and follow their own sweet will. And they mustn't be spoken to, or pulled up—for have they not kindly volunteered, and are they not giving their days for naught? These persons are the bane of the enterprises in which they condescend to meddle. Now, there is a vast deal too much of the gentleman-at-large about one's brain. One's brain has no right whatever to behave as a gentleman-at-large; but it in fact does. It forgets; it flatly ignores orders; at the critical moment, when pressure is highest, it simply lights a cigarette and goes out for a walk. And we meekly sit down under this behaviour! "I didn't feel like stewing," says the young man who, against his wish, will fail in his examination. "The words were out of my mouth before I knew it," says the husband whose wife is a woman. "I couldn't get any inspiration to-day," says the artist. "I can't resist Stilton," says the fellow who is dying of greed. "One can't help one's thoughts," says the old worrier. And this last really voices the secret excuse of all five.

And you all say to me: "My brain is myself. How can I alter myself? I was born like that." In the first place you were not born "like that," you have lapsed to that. And in the second place your brain is not yourself. It is only a part of yourself, and not the highest seat of authority. Do you love your mother, wife, or children with your brain? Do you desire with your brain? Do you, in a word, ultimately and essentially *live* with your brain? No. Your brain is an instrument. The proof that it is an instrument lies in the fact that, when extreme necessity urges, *you* can command your brain to do certain things, and it does them. The first of the two great principles which underlie the efficiency of the human machine is this: *The brain is a servant, exterior to the central force of the Ego.* If it is out of control the reason is not that it is uncontrollable, but merely that its discipline has been neglected. The brain can be trained, as the hand and eye can be trained; it can be made as obedient as a sporting dog, and by similar methods. In the meantime the indispensable preparation for brain-discipline is to form the habit of regarding one's brain as an instrument exterior to one's self, like a tongue or a foot.

IV

THE FIRST PRACTICAL STEP

The brain is a highly quaint organism. Let me say at once, lest I should be cannonaded by physiologists, psychologists, or metaphysicians, that by the "brain" I mean the faculty which reasons and which gives orders to the muscles. I mean exactly what the plain man means by the brain. The brain is the diplomatist which arranges relations between our instinctive self and the universe, and it fulfils its mission when it provides for the maximum of freedom to the instincts with the minimum of friction. It argues with the instincts. It takes them on one side and points out the unwisdom of certain performances. It catches them by the coat-tails when they are about to make fools of themselves. "Don't drink all that iced champagne at a draught," it says to one instinct; "we may die of it." "Don't catch that rude fellow one in the eye," it says to another instinct; "he is more powerful than us." It is, in fact, a majestic spectacle of common sense. And yet it has the most extraordinary lapses. It is just like that man—we all know him and consult him—who is a continual fount of excellent, sagacious advice on everything, but who somehow cannot bring his sagacity to bear on his own personal career.

In the matter of its own special activities the brain is usually undisciplined and unreliable. We never know what it will do next. We give it some work to do, say, as we are walking along the street to the office. Perhaps it has to devise some scheme for making £150 suffice for £200, or perhaps it has to plan out the heads of a very important letter. We meet a pretty woman, and away that undisciplined, sagacious brain runs after her, dropping the scheme or the draft letter, and amusing itself with aspirations or regrets for half an hour, an hour, sometimes a day. The serious part of our instinctive self feebly remonstrates, but without effect. Or it may be that we have suffered a great disappointment, which is definite and hopeless. Will the brain, like a sensible creature, leave that disappointment alone, and instead of living in the past live in the present or the future? Not it! Though it knows perfectly well that it is wasting its time and casting a very painful and utterly unnecessary gloom over itself and us, it can so little control its unhealthy morbid appetite that no expostulations will induce it to behave rationally. Or perhaps, after a confabulation with the soul, it has been decided that when next a certain harmful instinct comes into play the brain shall firmly interfere. "Yes," says the brain, "I really will watch that." But when the moment arrives, is the brain on the spot? The brain has probably forgotten the affair entirely, or remembered it too late; or sighs, as the victorious instinct knocks it on the head: "Well, *next* time!"

All this, and much more that every reader can supply from his own exciting souvenirs, is absurd and ridiculous on the part of the brain. It is a conclusive proof that the brain is out of condition, idle as a nigger, capricious as an actor-manager, and eaten to the core with loose habits. Therefore the brain must be put into training. It is the most important part of the human machine by which the soul expresses and develops itself, and it must learn good habits. And primarily it must be taught obedience. Obedience can only be taught by imposing one's will, by the sheer force of volition. And the brain must be mastered by will-power. The beginning of wise living lies in the control of the brain by the will; so that the brain may act according to the precepts which the brain itself gives. With an obedient disciplined brain a man may live always right up to the standard of his best moments.

To teach a child obedience you tell it to do something, and you see that that something is done. The same with the brain. Here is the foundation of an efficient life and the antidote for the tendency to make a fool of oneself. It is marvellously simple.

Say to your brain: "From 9 o'clock to 9.30 this morning you must dwell without ceasing on a particular topic which I will give you." Now, it doesn't matter what this topic is—the point is to control and invigorate the brain by exercise—but you may just as well give it a useful topic to think over as a futile one. You might give it this: "My brain is my servant. I am not the plaything of my brain." Let it concentrate on these statements for thirty minutes. "What?" you cry. "Is this the way to an efficient life? Why, there's nothing in it!" Simple as it may appear, this *is* the way, and it is the only way. As for there being nothing in it, try it. I guarantee that you will fail to keep your brain concentrated on the given idea for thirty seconds—let alone thirty minutes. You will find your brain conducting itself in a manner which would be comic were it not tragic. Your first experiments will result in disheartening failure, for to exact from the brain, at will and by will, concentration on a given idea for even so short a period as half an hour is an exceedingly difficult feat—and a fatiguing! It needs perseverance. It needs a terrible obstinacy on the part of the will. That brain of yours will be hopping about all over the place, and every time it hops you must bring it back by force to its original position. You must absolutely compel it to ignore every idea except the one which you have selected for its attention. You cannot hope to triumph all at once. But you can hope to triumph. There is no royal road to the control of the brain. There is no patent dodge about it, and no complicated function which a plain person may not comprehend. It is simply a question of: "I will, *I* will, and I *will*." (Italics here are indispensable.)

Let me resume. Efficient living, living up to one's best standard, getting the last ounce of power out of the machine with the minimum of friction: these things depend on the disciplined and vigorous condition of the brain. The brain can be disciplined by learning the habit of obedience. And it can learn the habit of obedience by the practice of concentration. Disciplinary concentration, though nothing could have the air of being simpler, is the basis of the whole structure. This fact must be grasped imaginatively; it must be seen and felt. The more regularly concentration is practised, the more firmly will the imagination grasp the effects of it, both direct and indirect. After but a few days of honest trying in the exercise which I have indicated, you will perceive its influence. You will grow accustomed to the idea, at first strange in its novelty, of the brain being external to the supreme force which is *you*, and in subjection to that force. You will, as a not very distant possibility, see yourself in possession of the power to switch your brain on and off in a particular subject as you switch electricity on and off in a particular room. The brain will get used to the straight paths of obedience. And—a remarkable phenomenon—it will, by the mere practice of obedience, become less forgetful and more effective. It will not so frequently give way to an instinct that takes it by surprise. In a word, it will have received a general tonic. With a brain that is improving every day you can set about the perfecting of the machine in a scientific manner.

V

Habit-Forming by Concentration

As soon as the will has got the upper hand of the brain—as soon as it can say to the brain, with a fair certainty of being obeyed: "Do this. Think along these lines, and continue to do so without wandering until I give you leave to stop"—then is the time arrived when the perfecting of the human machine may be undertaken in a large and comprehensive spirit, as a city council undertakes the purification and reconstruction of a city. The tremendous possibilities of an obedient brain will be perceived immediately we begin to reflect upon what we mean by our "character." Now, a person's character is, and can be, nothing else but the total result of his habits of thought. A person is benevolent because he habitually thinks benevolently. A person is idle because his thoughts dwell habitually on the instant pleasures of idleness. It is true that everybody is born with certain predispositions, and that these predispositions influence very strongly the early formation of habits of thought. But the fact remains that the character is built by long-continued habits of thought. If the mature edifice of character usually shows in an exaggerated form the peculiarities of the original predisposition, this merely indicates a probability that the slow erection of the edifice has proceeded at haphazard, and that reason has not presided over it. A child may be born with a tendency to bent shoulders. If nothing is done, if on the contrary he becomes a clerk and abhors gymnastics, his shoulders will develop an excessive roundness, entirely through habit. Whereas, if his will, guided by his reason, had compelled the formation of a corrective physical habit, his shoulders might have been, if not quite straight, nearly so. Thus a physical habit! The same with a mental habit.

The more closely we examine the development of original predispositions, the more clearly we shall see that this development is not inevitable, is not a process which works itself out independently according to mysterious, ruthless laws which we cannot understand. For instance, the effect of an original predisposition may be destroyed by an accidental shock. A young man with an inherited tendency to alcohol may develop into a stern teetotaller through the shock caused by seeing his drunken father strike his mother; whereas, if his father had chanced to be affectionate in drink, the son might have ended in the gutter. No ruthless law here! It is notorious, also, that natures are sometimes completely changed in their development by chance momentary contact with natures stronger than themselves. "From that day I resolved—" etc. You know the phrase. Often the resolve is not kept; but often it is kept. A spark has inflamed the will. The burning will has tyrannised over the brain. New habits have been formed. And the result looks just like a miracle.

Now, if these great transformations can be brought about by accident, cannot similar transformations be brought about by a reasonable design? At any rate, if one starts to bring them about, one starts with the assurance that transformations are not impossible, since they have occurred. One starts also in the full knowledge of the influence of habit on life. Take any one of your own habits, mental or physical. You will be able to recall the time when that habit did not exist, or if it did exist it was scarcely perceptible. And you will discover that nearly all your habits have been formed unconsciously, by daily repetitions which bore no relation to a general plan, and which you practised not noticing. You will be compelled to admit that your "character," as it is to-day, is a structure that has been built almost without the aid of an architect; higgledy-piggledy, anyhow. But occasionally the architect did step in and design something. Here and there among your habits you will find one that you consciously and of deliberate purpose initiated and perse-

vered with—doubtless owing to some happy influence. What is
the difference between that conscious habit and the unconscious habits? None whatever as regards its effect on the sum of
your character. It may be the strongest of all your habits. The
only quality that differentiates it from the others is that it has a
definite object (most likely a good object), and that it wholly or
partially fulfils that object. There is not a man who reads these
lines but has, in this detail or that, proved in himself that the
will, forcing the brain to repeat the same action again and again,
can modify the shape of his character as a sculptor modifies the
shape of damp clay.

But if a grown man's character is developing from day to day
(as it is), if nine-tenths of the development is due to unconscious
action and one-tenth to conscious action, and if the one-tenth
conscious is the most satisfactory part of the total result; why, in
the name of common sense, henceforward, should not nine-
tenths, instead of one-tenth, be due to conscious action? What
is there to prevent this agreeable consummation? There is nothing whatever to prevent it—except insubordination on the part
of the brain. And insubordination of the brain can be cured, as
I have previously shown. When I see men unhappy and ineffi-
cient in the craft of *living*, from sheer, crass inattention to their
own development; when I see misshapen men building up businesses and empires, and never stopping to build up themselves;
when I see dreary men expending precisely the same energy on
teaching a dog to walk on its hind-legs as would brighten the
whole colour of their own lives, I feel as if I wanted to give up
the ghost, so ridiculous, so fatuous does the spectacle seem! But,
of course, I do not give up the ghost. The paroxysm passes. Only
I really must cry out: "Can't you see what you're missing? Can't
you see that you're missing the most interesting thing on earth,
far more interesting than businesses, empires, and dogs?
Doesn't it strike you how clumsy and short-sighted you are—
working always with an inferior machine when you might have
a smooth-gliding perfection? Doesn't it strike you how badly you
are treating yourself?"

Listen, you confirmed grumbler, you who make the evening
meal hideous with complaints against destiny—for it is you I will

single out. Are you aware what people are saying about you behind your back? They are saying that you render yourself and your family miserable by the habit which has grown on you of always grumbling. "Surely it isn't as bad as that?" you protest. Yes, it is just as bad as that. You say: "The fact is, I know it's absurd to grumble. But I'm like that. I've tried to stop it, and I can't!" How have you tried to stop it? "Well, I've made up my mind several times to fight against it, but I never succeed. This is strictly between ourselves. I don't usually admit that I'm a grumbler." Considering that you grumble for about an hour and a half every day of your life, it was sanguine, my dear sir, to expect to cure such a habit by means of a solitary intention, formed at intervals in the brain and then forgotten. No! You must do more than that. If you will daily fix your brain firmly for half an hour on the truth (you know it to be a truth) that grumbling is absurd and futile, your brain will henceforward begin to form a habit in that direction; it will begin to be moulded to the idea that grumbling is absurd and futile. In odd moments, when it isn't thinking of anything in particular, it will suddenly remember that grumbling is absurd and futile. When you sit down to the meal and open your mouth to say: "I can't think what my ass of a partner means by——" it will remember that grumbling is absurd and futile, and will alter the arrangement of your throat, teeth, and tongue, so that you will say: "What fine weather we're having!" In brief, it will remember involuntarily, by a new habit. All who look into their experience will admit that the failure to replace old habits by new ones is due to the fact that at the critical moment the brain does not remember; it simply forgets. The practice of concentration will cure that. All depends on regular concentration. This grumbling is an instance, though chosen not quite at hazard.

VI

LORD OVER THE NODDLE

Having proved by personal experiment the truth of the first of the two great principles which concern the human machine—namely, that the brain is a servant, not a master, and can be controlled—we may now come to the second. The second is more fundamental than the first, but it can be of no use until the first is understood and put into practice. The human machine is an apparatus of brain and muscle for enabling the Ego to develop freely in the universe by which it is surrounded, without friction. Its function is to convert the facts of the universe to the best advantage of the Ego. The facts of the universe are the material with which it is its business to deal—not the facts of an ideal universe, but the facts of this universe. Hence, when friction occurs, when the facts of the universe cease to be of advantage to the Ego, the fault is in the machine. It is not the solar system that has gone wrong, but the human machine. Second great principle, therefore: *"In case of friction, the machine is always at fault."*

You can control nothing but your own mind. Even your two-year-old babe may defy you by the instinctive force of its personality. But your own mind you can control. Your own mind is a sacred enclosure into which nothing harmful can enter except by your permission. Your own mind has the power to transmute every external phenomenon to its own purposes. If happiness arises from cheerfulness, kindliness, and rectitude (and who will deny it?), what possible combination of circumstances is going to make you unhappy so long as the machine remains in order?

If self-development consists in the utilisation of one's environment (not utilisation of somebody else's environment), how can your environment prevent you from developing? You would look rather foolish without it, anyway. In that noddle of yours is everything necessary for development, for the maintaining of dignity, for the achieving of happiness, and you are absolute lord over the noddle, will you but exercise the powers of lordship. Why worry about the contents of somebody else's noddle, in which you can be nothing but an intruder, when you may arrive at a better result, with absolute certainty, by confining your activities to your own? "Look within." "The Kingdom of Heaven is within you." "Oh, yes!" you protest. "All that's old. Epictetus said that. Marcus Aurelius said that. Christ said that." They did. I admit it readily. But if you were ruffled this morning because your motor-omnibus broke down, and you had to take a cab, then so far as you are concerned these great teachers lived in vain. You, calling yourself a reasonable man, are going about dependent for your happiness, dignity, and growth, upon a thousand things over which you have no control, and the most exquisitely organised machine for ensuring happiness, dignity, and growth, is rusting away inside you. And all because you have a sort of notion that a saying said two thousand years ago cannot be practical.

You remark sagely to your child: "No, my child, you cannot have that moon, and you will accomplish nothing by crying for it. Now, here is this beautiful box of bricks, by means of which you may amuse yourself while learning many wonderful matters and improving your mind. You must try to be content with what you have, and to make the best of it. If you had the moon you wouldn't be any happier." Then you lie awake half the night repining because the last post has brought a letter to the effect that "the Board cannot entertain your application for," etc. You say the two cases are not alike. They are not. Your child has never heard of Epictetus. On the other hand, justice *is* the moon. At your age you surely know that. "But the Directors *ought* to have granted my application," you insist. Exactly! I agree. But we are not in a universe of *oughts*. You have a special apparatus within you for dealing with a universe where *oughts* are flagrantly disregarded. And you are not using it. You are lying awake, keeping your wife awake, injuring your health, injuring hers, losing your dignity and your cheerfulness. Why? Because you think that these antics and performances will influence the Board? Because you think that they will put you into a better condition for dealing with your environment to-morrow? Not a bit. Simply because the machine is at fault.

In certain cases we do make use of our machines (as well as their sad condition of neglect will allow), but in other cases we behave in an extraordinarily irrational manner. Thus if we sally out and get caught in a heavy shower we do not, unless very far gone in foolishness, sit down and curse the weather. We put up our umbrella, if we have one, and if not we hurry home. We may grumble, but it is not serious grumbling; we accept the shower as a fact of the universe, and control ourselves. Thus also, if by a sudden catastrophe we lose somebody who is important to us, we grieve, but we control ourselves, recognising one of those hazards of destiny from which not even millionaires are exempt. And the result on our Ego is usually to improve it in essential respects. But there are other strokes of destiny, other facts of the universe, against which we protest as a child protests when deprived of the moon.

Take the case of an individual with an imperfect idea of honesty. Now, that individual is the consequence of his father and mother and his environment, and his father and mother of theirs, and so backwards to the single-celled protoplasm. That individual is a result of the cosmic order, the inevitable product of cause and effect. We know that. We must admit that he is just as much a fact of the universe as a shower of rain or a storm at sea that swallows a ship. We freely grant in the abstract that there must be, at the present stage of evolution, a certain number of persons with unfair minds. We are quite ready to contemplate such an individual with philosophy—until it happens that, in the course of the progress of the solar system, he runs up against ourselves. Then listen to the outcry! Listen to the continual explosions of a righteous man aggrieved! The individual may be our clerk, cashier, son, father, brother, partner, wife, employer. We are ill-used! We are being treated unfairly! We kick; we scream. We nourish the inward sense of grievance that eats the core out of content. We sit down in the rain. We decline to think of umbrellas, or to run to shelter.

We care not that that individual is a fact which the universe has been slowly manufacturing for millions of years. Our attitude implies that we want eternity to roll back and begin again, in such wise that we at any rate shall not be disturbed. Though we have a machine for the transmutation of facts into food for our growth, we do not dream of using it. But, we say, he is doing us harm! Where? In our minds. He has robbed us of our peace, our comfort, our happiness, our good temper. Even if he has, we might just as well inveigh against a shower. But has he? What was our brain doing while this naughty person stepped in and robbed us of the only possessions worth having? No, no! It is not that he has done us harm—the one cheerful item in a universe of stony facts is that no one can harm anybody except himself— it is merely that we have been silly, precisely as silly as if we had taken a seat in the rain with a folded umbrella by our side. . . . The machine is at fault. I fancy we are now obtaining glimpses of what that phrase really means.

VII

What "Living" Chiefly Is

It is in intercourse—social, sentimental, or business—with one's fellows that the qualities and the condition of the human machine are put to the test and strained. That part of my life which I conduct by myself, without reference—or at any rate without direct reference—to others, I can usually manage in such a way that the gods do not positively weep at the spectacle thereof. My environment is simpler, less puzzling, when I am alone, my calm and my self-control less liable to violent fluctuations. Impossible to be disturbed by a chair! Impossible that a chair should get on one's nerves! Impossible to blame a chair for not being as reasonable, as archangelic as I am myself! But when it comes to people! . . . Well, that is "living," then! The art of life, the art of extracting all its power from the human machine, does not lie chiefly in processes of bookish-culture, nor in contemplations of the beauty and majesty of existence. It lies chiefly in keeping the peace, the whole peace, and nothing but the peace, with those with whom one is "thrown." Is it in sitting ecstatic over Shelley, Shakespeare, or Herbert Spencer, solitary in my room of a night, that I am "improving myself" and learning to live? Or is it in watching over all my daily human contacts? Do not seek to escape the comparison by insinuating that I despise study, or by pointing out that the eternal verities are beyond dailiness. Nothing of the kind! I am so "silly" about books that merely to possess them gives me pleasure. And if the verities are good for eternity they ought to be good for a day. If I cannot exchange them for daily coin—if I can't buy happiness

for a single day because I've nothing less than an eternal verity
about me and nobody has sufficient change—then my eternal
verity is not an eternal verity. It is merely an unnegotiable bit of
glass (called a diamond), or even a note on the Bank of
Engraving.

I can say to myself when I arise in the morning: "I am master
of my brain. No one can get in there and rage about like a bull
in a china shop. If my companions on the planet's crust choose
to rage about they cannot affect *me*! I will not let them. I have
power to maintain my own calm, and I will. No earthly being
can force me to be false to my principles, or to be blind to the
beauty of the universe, or to be gloomy, or to be irritable, or to
complain against my lot. For these things depend on the brain;
cheerfulness, kindliness, and honest thinking are all within the
department of the brain. The disciplined brain can accomplish
them. And my brain is disciplined, and I will discipline it more
and more as the days pass. I am, therefore, independent of hazard, and I will back myself to conduct all intercourse as becomes
a rational creature." . . . I can say this. I can ram this argument
by force of will into my brain, and by dint of repeating it often
enough I shall assuredly arrive at the supreme virtues of reason.
I should assuredly conquer—the brain being such a machine of
habit—even if I did not take the trouble to consider in the
slightest degree what manner of things my fellow-men are—by
acting merely in my own interests. But the way of perfection (I
speak relatively) will be immensely shortened and smoothed if I
do consider, dispassionately, the case of the other human
machines. Thus:—

The truth is that my attitude towards my fellows is funda-
mentally and totally wrong, and that it entails on my thinking
machine a strain which is quite unnecessary, though I may have
arranged the machine so as to withstand the strain successfully.
The secret of smooth living is a calm cheerfulness which will
leave me always in full possession of my reasoning faculty—in
order that I may live by reason instead of by instinct and
momentary passion. The secret of calm cheerfulness is kindliness; no person can be consistently cheerful and calm who does
not consistently think kind thoughts. But how can I be kindly

when I pass the major portion of my time in blaming the people who surround me—who are part of my environment? If I, blaming, achieve some approach to kindliness, it is only by a great and exhausting effort of self-mastery. The inmost secret, then, lies in not blaming, in not judging and emitting verdicts. Oh! I do not blame by word of mouth! I am far too advanced for such a puerility. I keep the blame in my own breast, where it festers. I am always privately forgiving, which is bad for me. Because, you know, there is nothing to forgive. I do not have to forgive bad weather; nor, if I found myself in an earthquake, should I have to forgive the earthquake.

All blame, uttered or unexpressed, is wrong. I do not blame myself. I can explain myself to myself. I can invariably explain myself. If I forged a friend's name on a cheque I should explain the affair quite satisfactorily to myself. And instead of blaming myself I should sympathise with myself for having been driven into such an excessively awkward corner. Let me examine honestly my mental processes, and I must admit that my attitude towards others is entirely different from my attitude towards myself. I must admit that in the seclusion of my mind, though I say not a word, I am constantly blaming others because I am not happy. Whenever I bump up against an opposing personality and my smooth progress is impeded, I secretly blame the opposer. I act as though I had shouted to the world: "Clear out of the way, everyone, for *I* am coming!" Everyone does not clear out of the way. I did not really expect everyone to clear out of the way. But I act, within, as though I had so expected. I blame. Hence kindliness, hence cheerfulness, is rendered vastly more difficult for me.

What I ought to do is this! I ought to reflect again and again, and yet again, that the beings among whom I have to steer, the living environment out of which I have to manufacture my happiness, are just as inevitable in the scheme of evolution as I am myself; have just as much right to be themselves as I have to be myself; are precisely my equals in the face of Nature; are capable of being explained as I am capable of being explained; are entitled to the same latitude as I am entitled to, and are no more responsible for their composition and their environment than I for mine. I ought to reflect again and again, and yet again, that they all deserve from me as much sympathy as I give to myself. Why not? Having thus reflected in a general manner, I ought to take one by one the individuals with whom I am brought into frequent contact, and seek, by a deliberate effort of the imagination and the reason, to understand them, to understand why they act thus and thus, what their difficulties are, what their "explanation" is, and how friction can be avoided. So I ought to reflect, morning after morning, until my brain is saturated with the cases of these individuals. Here is a course of discipline. If I follow it I shall gradually lose the preposterous habit of blaming, and I shall have laid the foundations of that quiet, unshakable self-possession which is the indispensable preliminary of conduct according to reason, of thorough efficiency in the machine of happiness. But something in me, something distinctly base, says: "Yes. The put-yourself-in-his-place business over again! The do-unto-others business over again!" Just so! Something in me is ashamed of being "moral." (You all know the feeling!) Well, morals are naught but another name for reasonable conduct; a higher and more practical form of egotism—an egotism which, while freeing others, frees myself. I have tried the lower form of egotism. And it has failed. If I am afraid of being moral, if I prefer to cut off my nose to spite my face, well, I must accept the consequences. But truth will prevail.

VIII

THE DAILY FRICTION

It is with common daily affairs that I am now dealing, not with heroic enterprises, ambitions, martyrdoms. Take the day, the ordinary day in the ordinary house or office. Though it comes seven times a week, and is the most banal thing imaginable, it is quite worth attention. How does the machine get through it? Ah! the best that can be said of the machine is that it does get through it, somehow. The friction, though seldom such as to bring matters to a standstill, is frequent—the sort of friction that, when it occurs in a bicycle, is just sufficient to annoy the rider, but not sufficient to make him get off the machine and examine the bearings. Occasionally the friction is very loud; indeed, disturbing, and at rarer intervals it shrieks, like an omnibus brake out of order. You know those days when you have the sensation that life is not large enough to contain the household or the office-staff, when the business of intercourse may be compared to the manœuvres of two people who, having awakened with a bad headache, are obliged to dress simultaneously in a very small bedroom. "After you with that towel!" in accents of bitter, grinding politeness. "If you could kindly move your things off this chair!" in a voice that would blow brains out if it were a bullet. I venture to say that you know those days. "But," you reply, "such days are few. Usually . . . !" Well, usually, the friction, though less intense, is still proceeding. We grow accustomed to it. We scarcely notice it, as a person in a stuffy chamber will scarcely notice the stuffiness. But the deteriorating influence due to friction goes on, even if unperceived. And one morning we perceive its ravages—and write a letter to the *Telegraph* to inquire whether life is worth living, or whether marriage is a failure, or whether men are more polite than women. The proof that friction, in various and varying degrees, is practically continuous in most households lies in the fact that when we chance on a household where there is no friction we are startled. We can't recover from the phenomenon. And in describing this household to our friends, we say: "They get on so well together," as if we were saying: "They have wings and can fly! Just fancy! Did you ever hear of such a thing?"

Ninety per cent of all daily friction is caused by tone—mere tone of voice. Try this experiment. Say: "Oh, you little darling, you sweet pet, you entirely charming creature!" to a baby or a dog; but roar these delightful epithets in the tone of saying: "You infernal little nuisance! If I hear another sound I'll break every bone in your body!" The baby will infallibly whimper, and the dog will infallibly mouch off. True, a dog is not a human being, neither is a baby. They cannot understand. It is precisely because they cannot understand and articulate words that the experiment is valuable; for it separates the effect of the tone from the effect of the words spoken. He who speaks, speaks twice. His words convey his thought, and his tone conveys his mental attitude towards the person spoken to. And certainly the attitude, so far as friction goes, is more important than the thought. Your wife may say to you: "I shall buy that hat I spoke to you about." And you may reply, quite sincerely, "As you please." But it will depend on your tone whether you convey: "As you please. I am sympathetically anxious that your innocent caprices should be indulged." Or whether you convey: "As you please. Only don't bother me with hats. I am above hats. A great deal too much money is spent in this house on hats. However, I'm helpless!" Or whether you convey: "As you please, heart of my heart, but if you would like to be a nice girl, go gently. We're rather tight." I need not elaborate. I am sure of being comprehended.

As tone is the expression of attitude, it is, of course, caused by attitude. The frictional tone is chiefly due to that general attitude of blame which I have already condemned as being absurd and unjustifiable. As, by constant watchful discipline, we gradually lose this silly attitude of blame, so the tone will of itself gradually change. But the two ameliorations can proceed together, and it is a curious thing that an agreeable tone, artificially and deliberately adopted, will influence the mental attitude almost as much as the mental attitude will influence the tone. If you honestly feel resentful against someone, but, having understood the foolishness of fury, intentionally mask your fury under a persuasive tone, your fury will at once begin to abate. You will be led into a rational train of thought; you will see that after all the object of your resentment has a right to exist, and that he is neither a doormat nor a scoundrel, and that anyhow nothing is to be gained, and much is to be lost, by fury. You will see that fury is unworthy of you.

Do you remember the gentleness of the tone which you employed after the healing of your first quarrel with a beloved companion? Do you remember the persuasive tone which you used when you wanted to obtain something from a difficult person on whom your happiness depended? Why should not your tone always combine these qualities? Why should you not carefully school your tone? Is it beneath you to ensure the largest possible amount of your own "way" by the simplest means? Or is there at the back of your mind that peculiarly English and German idea that politeness, sympathy, and respect for another immortal soul would imply deplorable weakness on your part? You say that your happiness does not depend on every person whom you happen to speak to. Yes, it does. Your happiness is always dependent on just that person. Produce friction, and you suffer. Idle to argue that the person has no business to be upset by your tone! You have caused avoidable friction, simply because your machine for dealing with your environment was suffering from pride, ignorance, or thoughtlessness. You say I am making a mountain out of a mole-hill. No! I am making a mountain out of ten million mole-hills. And that is what life does. It is the little but continuous causes that have great effects. I repeat: Why not deliberately adopt a gentle, persuasive tone— just to see what the results are? Surely you are not ashamed to be wise. You may smile superiorly as you read this. Yet you know very well that more than once you *have* resolved to use a gentle and persuasive tone on all occasions, and that the sole reason why you had that fearful shindy yesterday with your cousin's sister-in-law was that you had long since failed to keep your resolve. But you were of my mind once, and more than once.

What you have to do is to teach the new habit to your brain by daily concentration on it; by forcing your brain to think of nothing else for half an hour of a morning. After a time the brain will begin to remember automatically. For, of course, the explanation of your previous failures is that your brain, undisciplined, merely forgot at the critical moment. The tone was out of your mouth before your brain had waked up. It is necessary to watch, as though you were a sentinel, not only against the wrong tone, but against the other symptoms of the attitude of blame. Such as the frown. It is necessary to regard yourself constantly, and in minute detail. You lie in bed for half an hour and enthusiastically concentrate on this beautiful new scheme of the right tone. You rise, and because you don't achieve a proper elegance of necktie at the first knotting, you frown and swear and clench your teeth! There is a symptom of the wrong attitude towards your environment. You are awake, but your brain isn't. It is in such a symptom that you may judge yourself. And not a trifling symptom, either! If you will frown at a necktie, if you will use language to a necktie which no gentleman should use to a necktie, what will you be capable of to a responsible being? . . . Yes, it is very difficult. But it can be done.

IX

"Fire!"

In this business of daily living, of ordinary usage of the machine in hourly intercourse, there occurs sometimes a phenomenon which is the cause of a great deal of trouble, and the result of a very ill-tended machine. It is a phenomenon impossible to ignore, and yet, so shameful is it, so degrading, so shocking, so miserable, that I hesitate to mention it. For one class of reader is certain to ridicule me, loftily saying: "One really doesn't expect to find this sort of thing in print nowadays!" And another class of reader is certain to get angry. Nevertheless, as one of my main objects in the present book is to discuss matters which "people don't talk about," I shall discuss this matter. But my diffidence in doing so is such that I must approach it deviously, describing it first by means of a figure.

Imagine that, looking at a man's house, you suddenly perceive it to be on fire. The flame is scarcely perceptible. You could put it out if you had a free hand. But you have not got a free hand. It is his house, not yours. He may or may not know that his house is burning. You are aware by experience, however, that if you directed his attention to the flame, the effect of your warning would be exceedingly singular, almost incredible. For the effect would be that he would instantly begin to strike matches, pour on petroleum, and fan the flame, violently resenting interference. Therefore you can only stand and watch, hoping that he will notice the flames before they are beyond control, and extinguish them. The probability is, however, that he will notice the flames too late. And, powerless to avert disaster, you are condemned, therefore, to watch the damage of valuable property. The flames leap higher and higher, and they do not die down till they have burned themselves out. You avert your gaze from the spectacle, and until you are gone the owner of the house pretends that nothing has occurred. When alone, he curses himself for his carelessness.

The foregoing is meant to be a description of what happens when a man passes through the incendiary experience known as "losing his temper." (There! the cat of my chapter is out of the bag!) A man who has lost his temper is simply being "burnt out." His constitutes one of the most curious and (for everybody) humiliating spectacles that life offers. It is an insurrection, a boiling-over, a sweeping storm. Dignity, common sense, justice are shrivelled up and destroyed. Anarchy reigns. The devil has broken his chain. Instinct is stamping on the face of reason. And in that man civilisation has temporarily receded millions of years. Of course, the thing amounts to a nervous disease, and I think it is almost universal. You at once protest that you never lose your temper—haven't lost your temper for ages! But do you not mean that you have not smashed furniture for ages? These fires are of varying intensities. Some of them burn very dully. Yet they burn. One man loses his temper; another is merely "ruffled." But the event is the same in kind. When you are "ruffled," when you are conscious of a resentful vibration that surprises all your being, when your voice changes, when you notice a change in the demeanour of your companion, who sees that he has "touched a tender point," you may not go to the length of smashing furniture, but you have had a fire, and your dignity is damaged. You admit it to yourself afterwards. I am sure you know what I mean. And I am nearly sure that you, with your courageous candour, will admit that from time to time you suffer from these mysterious "fires."

"Temper," one of the plagues of human society, is generally held to be incurable, save by the vague process of exercising self-control—a process which seldom has any beneficial results. It is regarded now as smallpox used to be regarded—as a visitation of Providence, which must be borne. But I do not hold it to be incurable. I am convinced that it is permanently curable. And its eminent importance as a nuisance to mankind at large deserves, I think, that it should receive particular attention. Anyhow, I am strongly against the visitation of Providence theory, as being unscientific, primitive, and conducive to unashamed *laissez-aller.* A man can be master in his own house. If he cannot be master by simple force of will, he can be master by ruse and wile. I would employ cleverness to maintain the throne of reason when it is likely to be upset in the mind by one of these devastating and disgraceful insurrections of brute instinct.

It is useless for a man in the habit of losing or mislaying his temper to argue with himself that such a proceeding is folly, that it serves no end, and does nothing but harm. It is useless for him to argue that in allowing his temper to stray he is probably guilty of cruelty, and certainly guilty of injustice to those persons who are forced to witness the loss. It is useless for him to argue that a man of uncertain temper in a house is like a man who goes about a house with a loaded revolver sticking from his pocket, and that all considerations of fairness and reason have to be subordinated in that house to the fear of the revolver, and that such peace as is maintained in that house is often a shameful and an unjust peace. These arguments will not be strong enough to prevail against one of the most powerful and capricious of all habits. This habit must be met and conquered (and it *can* be!) by an even more powerful quality in the human mind; I mean the universal human horror of looking ridiculous. The man who loses his temper often thinks he is doing something rather fine and majestic. On the contrary, so far is this from being the fact, he is merely making an ass of himself. He is merely parading himself as an undignified fool, as that supremely contemptible figure— a grown-up baby. He may intimidate a feeble companion by his raging, or by the dark sullenness of a more subdued flame, but in the heart of even the weakest companion is a bedrock feeling of contempt for him. The way in which a man of uncertain temper is treated by his friends proves that they despise him, for they do not treat him as a reasonable being. How should they treat him as a reasonable being when the tenure of his reason is so insecure? And if only he could hear what is said of him behind his back! . . .

The invalid can cure himself by teaching his brain the habit of dwelling upon his extreme fatuity. Let him concentrate regularly, with intense fixation, upon the ideas: "When I lose my temper, when I get ruffled, when that mysterious vibration runs through me, I am making a donkey of myself, a donkey, and a donkey! You understand, a preposterous donkey! I am behaving like a great baby. I look a fool. I am a spectacle bereft of dignity. Everybody despises me, smiles at me in secret, disdains the idiotic ass with whom it is impossible to reason."

Ordinarily the invalid disguises from himself this aspect of his disease, and his brain will instinctively avoid it as much as it can. But in hours of calm he can slowly and regularly force his brain, by the practice of concentration, to familiarise itself with just this aspect, so that in time its instinct will be to think first, and not last, of just this aspect. When he has arrived at that point he is saved. No man who, at the very inception of the fire, is visited with a clear vision of himself as an arrant ass and pitiable object of contempt, will lack the volition to put the fire out. But, be it noted, he will not succeed until he can do it at once. A fire is a fire, and the engines must gallop by themselves out of the station instantly. This means the acquirement of a mental habit. During the preliminary stages of the cure he should, of course, avoid inflammable situations. This is a perfectly simple thing to do, if the brain has been disciplined out of its natural forgetfulness.

X

MISCHIEVOUSLY OVERWORKING IT

I have dealt with the two general major causes of friction in the daily use of the machine. I will now deal with a minor cause, and make an end of merc dailiness. This minor cause—and after all I do not know that its results are so trifling as to justify the epithet "minor"—is the straining of the machine by forcing it to do work which it was never intended to do. Although we are incapable of persuading our machines to do effectively that which they are bound to do somehow, we continually overburden them with entirely unnecessary and inept tasks. We cannot, it would seem, let things alone.

For example, in the ordinary household the amount of machine horse-power expended in fighting for the truth is really quite absurd. This pure zeal for the establishment and general admission of the truth is usually termed "contradictoriness." But, of course, it is not that; it is something higher. My wife states that the Joneses have gone into a new flat, of which the rent is £165 a year. Now, Jones has told me personally that the rent of his new flat is £156 a year. I correct my wife. Knowing that she is in the right, she corrects me. She cannot bear that a falsehood should prevail. It is not a question of £9, it is a question of truth. Her enthusiasm for truth excites my enthusiasm for truth. Five minutes ago I didn't care twopence whether the rent of the Joneses' new flat was £165 or £156 or £1,056 a year. But now I care intensely that it is £156. I have formed myself into a select society for the propagating of the truth about the rent of the Joneses' new flat, and my wife has done the same. In eloquence, in argumentative skill, in strict supervision of our tempers, we each of us squander enormous quantities of that h.-p. which is so precious to us. And the net effect is naught.

Now, if one of us two had understood the elementary principles of human engineering, that one would have said (privately): "Truth is indestructible. Truth will out. Truth is never in a hurry. If it doesn't come out to-day it will come out to-morrow or next year. It can take care of itself. Ultimately my wife (or my husband) will learn the essential cosmic truth about the rent of the Joneses' new flat. I already know it, and the moment when she (or he) knows it also will be the moment of my triumph. She (or he) will not celebrate my triumph openly, but it will be none the less real. And my reputation for accuracy and calm restraint will be consolidated. If, by a rare mischance, I am in error, it will be vastly better for me in the day of my undoing that I have not been too positive now. Besides, nobody has appointed me sole custodian of the great truth concerning the rent of the Joneses' new flat. I was not brought into the world to be a safe-deposit, and more urgent matters summon me to effort." If one of us had meditated thus, much needless friction would have been avoided and power saved; *amour-propre* would not have been exposed to risks; the sacred cause of truth would not in the least have suffered; and the rent of the Joneses' new flat would anyhow have remained exactly what it is.

In addition to straining the machine by our excessive anxiety for the spread of truth, we give a very great deal too much attention to the state of other people's machines. I cannot too strongly, too sarcastically, deprecate this astonishing habit. It will be found to be rife in nearly every household and in nearly every office. We are most of us endeavouring to rearrange the mechanism in other heads than our own. This is always dangerous and generally futile. Considering the difficulty we have in our own brains, where our efforts are sure of being accepted as well-meant, and where we have at any rate a rough notion of the machine's construction, our intrepidity in adventuring among the delicate adjustments of other brains is remarkable. We are cursed by too much of the missionary spirit. We must needs voyage into the China of our brother's brain, and explain there that things are seriously wrong in that heathen land, and make ourselves unpleasant in the hope of getting them put right. We have all our own brain and body on which to wreak our personality, but this is not enough; we must extend our personality further, just as though we were a colonising world-power intoxicated by the idea of the "white man's burden."

One of the central secrets of efficient daily living is to leave our daily companions alone a great deal more than we do, and attend to ourselves. If a daily companion is conducting his life upon principles which you know to be false, and with results which you feel to be unpleasant, the safe rule is to keep your mouth shut. Or if, out of your singular conceit, you are compelled to open it, open it with all precautions, and with the formal politeness you would use to a stranger. Intimacy is no excuse for rough manners, though the majority of us seem to think it is. You are not in charge of the universe; you are in charge of yourself. You cannot hope to manage the universe in your spare time, and if you try you will probably make a mess of such part of the universe as you touch, while gravely neglecting yourself. In every family there is generally someone whose meddlesome interest in other machines leads to serious friction in his own. Criticise less, even in the secrecy of your chamber. And do not blame at all. Accept your environment and adapt yourself to it in silence, instead of noisily attempting to adapt your environment to yourself. Here is true wisdom. You have no business trespassing beyond the confines of your own individuality. In so trespassing you are guilty of impertinence. This is obvious. And yet one of the chief activities of home-life consists in prancing about at random on other people's private lawns. What I say applies even to the relation between parents and children. And though my precept is exaggerated, it is purposely exaggerated in order effectively to balance the exaggeration in the opposite direction.

All individualities, other than one's own, are part of one's environment. The evolutionary process is going on all right, and they are a portion of it. Treat them as inevitable. To assert that they are inevitable is not to assert that they are unalterable. Only the alteration of them is not primarily your affair; it is theirs. Your affair is to use them, as they are, without self-righteousness, blame, or complaint, for the smooth furtherance of your own ends. There is no intention here to rob them of responsibility by depriving them of free-will while saddling *you* with responsibility as a free agent. As your environment they must be accepted as inevitable, because they *are* inevitable. But as centres themselves they have their own responsibility: which is not yours. The historic question: "Have we free-will, or are we the puppets of determinism?" enters now. As a question it is fascinating and futile. It has never been, and it never will be, settled. The theory of determinism cannot be demolished by argument. But in his heart every man, including the most obstinate supporter of the theory, demolishes it every hour of every day. On the other hand, the theory of free-will can be demolished by ratiocination! So much the worse for ratiocination! *If we regard ourselves as free agents, and the personalities surrounding us as the puppets of determinism*, we shall have arrived at the working compromise from which the finest results of living can be obtained. The philosophic experience of centuries, if it has proved anything, has proved this. And the man who acts upon it in the common, banal contracts and collisions of the difficult experiment which we call daily life, will speedily become convinced of its practical worth.

XI

AN INTERLUDE

For ten chapters you have stood it, but not without protest. I
know the feeling which is in your minds, and which has
manifested itself in numerous criticisms of my ideas. That feeling may be briefly translated, perhaps, thus: "This is all very
well, but—it isn't true, not a bit! It's only a fairy-tale that you
have been telling us. Miracles don't happen," etc. I, on my part,
have a feeling that unless I take your feeling in hand at once,
and firmly deal with it, I had better put my shutters up, for you
will have got into the way of regarding me simply as a source of
idle amusement. Already I can perceive, from the expressions of
some critics, that, so far as they are concerned, I might just as
well not have written a word. Therefore at this point I pause, in
order to insist once more upon what I began by saying.

The burden of your criticism is: "Human nature is always the
same. I know my faults. But it is useless to tell me about them.
I can't alter them. I was born like that." The fatal weakness of
this argument is, first, that it is based on a complete falsity; and
second, that it puts you in an untenable position. Human nature
does change. Nothing can be more unscientific, more hopelessly
mediæval, than to imagine that it does not. It changes like everything else. You can't see it change. True! But then you can't see
the grass growing—not unless you arise very early.

Is human nature the same now as in the days of Babylonian
civilisation, when the social machine was oiled by drenchings of
blood? Is it the same now as in the days of Greek civilisation,
when there was no such thing as romantic love between the

sexes? Is it the same now as it was during the centuries when constant friction had to provide its own cure in the shape of constant war? Is it the same now as it was on March 2nd, 1819, when the British Government officially opposed a motion to consider the severity of the criminal laws (which included capital punishment for cutting down a tree, and other sensible dodges against friction), and were defeated by a majority of only nineteen votes? Is it the same now as in the year 1883, when the first S.P.C.C. was formed in England?

If you consider that human nature is still the same, you should instantly go out and make a bonfire of the works of Spencer, Darwin, and Wallace, and then return to enjoy the purely jocular side of the present volume. If you admit that it has changed, let me ask you how it has changed, unless by the continual infinitesimal efforts, *upon themselves*, of individual men, like you and me. Did you suppose it was changed by magic, or by acts of parliament, or by the action of groups on persons, and not of persons on groups? Let me tell you that human nature has changed since yesterday. Let me tell you that to-day reason has a more powerful voice in the directing of instinct than it had yesterday. Let me tell you that to-day the friction of the machines is less screechy and grinding than it was yesterday.

"You were born like that, and you can't alter yourself, and so it's no use talking." If you really believe this, why make any effort at all? Why not let the whole business beautifully slide and yield to your instincts? What object can there be in trying to control yourself in any manner whatever if you are unalterable? Assert yourself to be unalterable, and you assert yourself a fatalist. Assert yourself a fatalist, and you free yourself from all moral responsibility—and other people, too. Well, then, act up to your convictions, if convictions they are. If you can't alter yourself, I can't alter myself, and supposing that I come along and bash you on the head and steal your purse, you can't blame me. You can only, on recovering consciousness, affectionately grasp my hand and murmur: "Don't apologise, my dear fellow; we can't alter ourselves."

This, you say, is absurd. It is. That is one of my innumerable points. The truth is, you do not really believe that you cannot alter yourself. What is the matter with you is just what is the matter with me—sheer idleness. You hate getting up in the morning, and to excuse your inexcusable indolence you talk big about Fate. Just as "patriotism is the last refuge of a scoundrel," so fatalism is the last refuge of a shirker. But you deceive no one, least of all yourself. You have not, rationally, a leg to stand on. At this juncture, because I have made you laugh, you consent to say: "I do try, all I can. But I can only alter myself a very little. By constitution I am mentally idle. I can't help that, can I?" Well, so long as you are not the only absolutely unchangeable thing in a universe of change, I don't mind. It is something for you to admit that you can alter yourself even a very little. The difference between our philosophies is now only a question of degree.

In the application of any system of perfecting the machine, no two persons will succeed equally. From the disappointed tone of some of your criticisms it might be fancied that I had advertised a system for making archangels out of tailors' dummies. Such was not my hope. I have no belief in miracles. But I know that when a thing is thoroughly well done it often has the air of being a miracle. My sole aim is to insist that every man shall perfect his machine to the best of *his* powers, not to the best of somebody else's powers. I do not indulge in any hope that a man can be better than his best self. I am, however, convinced that every man fails to be his best self a great deal oftener than he need fail—for the reason that his will-power, be it great or small, is not directed according to the principles of common sense.

Common sense will surely lead a man to ask the question: "Why did my actions yesterday contradict my reason?" The reply to this question will nearly always be: "Because at the critical moment I forgot." The supreme explanation of the abortive results of so many efforts at self-alteration, the supreme explanation of our frequent miserable scurrying into a doctrine of fatalism, is simple forgetfulness. It is not force that we lack, but the skill to remember exactly what our reason would have us do or think at the moment itself. How is this skill to be acquired? It can only be acquired, as skill at games is acquired, by practice;

by the training of the organ involved to such a point that the organ acts rightly by instinct instead of wrongly by instinct. There are degrees of success in this procedure, but there is no such phenomenon as complete failure.

Habits which increase friction can be replaced by habits which lessen friction. Habits which arrest development can be replaced by habits which encourage development. And as a habit is formed naturally, so it can be formed artificially, by imitation of the unconscious process, by accustoming the brain to the new idea. Let me, as an example, refer again to the minor subject of daily friction, and, within that subject, to the influence of tone. A man employs a frictional tone through habit. The frictional tone is an instinct with him. But if he had a quarter of an hour to reflect before speaking, and if during that quarter of an hour he could always listen to arguments against the frictional tone, his use of the frictional tone would rapidly diminish; his reason would conquer his instinct. As things are, his instinct conquers his reason by a surprise attack, by taking it unawares. Regular daily concentration of the brain, for a certain period, upon the non-frictional tone, and the immense advantages of its use, will gradually set up in the brain a new habit of thinking about the non-frictional tone; until at length the brain, disciplined, turns to the correct act before the old, silly instinct can capture it; and ultimately a new sagacious instinct will supplant the old one.

This is the rationale. It applies to all habits. Any person can test its efficiency in any habit. I care not whether he be of strong or weak will—he can test it. He will soon see the tremendous difference between merely "making a good resolution"—(he has been doing that all his life without any very brilliant consequences)—and concentrating the brain for a given time exclusively upon a good resolution. Concentration, the efficient mastery of the brain—all is there!

XII

An Interest in Life

After a certain period of mental discipline, of deliberate habit-forming and habit-breaking, such as I have been indicating, a man will begin to acquire at any rate a superficial knowledge, a nodding acquaintance, with that wonderful and mysterious affair, his brain, and he will also begin to perceive how important a factor in daily life is the control of his brain. He will assuredly be surprised at the miracles which lie between his collar and his hat, in that queer box that he calls his head. For the effects that can be accomplished by mere steady, persistent thinking must appear to be miracles to apprentices in the practice of thought. When once a man, having passed an unhappy day because his clumsy, negligent brain forgot to control his instincts at a critical moment, has said to his brain: "I will force you, by concentrating you on that particular point, to act efficiently the next time similar circumstances arise," and when he has carried out his intention, and when the awkward circumstances have recurred, and his brain, disciplined, has done its work, and so prevented unhappiness—then that man will regard his brain with a new eye. "By Jove!" he will say; "I've stopped one source of unhappiness, anyway. There was a time when I should have made a fool of myself in a little domestic crisis such as to-day's. But I have gone safely through it. I am all right. She is all right. The atmosphere is not dangerous with undischarged electricity! And all because my brain, being in proper condition, watched firmly over my instincts! I must keep this up." He will peer into that brain more and more. He will see more and more of its possibilities. He will have a new and a supreme interest in *life*. A garden is a fairly interesting thing. But the cultivation of a garden is as dull as cold mutton compared to the cultivation of a brain; and wet weather won't interfere with digging, planting, and pruning in the box.

In due season the man whose hobby is his brain will gradually settle down into a daily routine, with which routine he will start the day. The idea at the back of the mind of the ordinary man (by the ordinary man I mean the man whose brain is not his hobby) is almost always this: "There are several things at present hanging over me—worries, unfulfilled ambitions, unrealised desires. As soon as these things are definitely settled, then I shall begin to live and enjoy myself." That is the ordinary man's usual idea. He has it from his youth to his old age. He is invariably waiting for something to happen before he really begins to live. I am sure that if you are an ordinary man (of course, you aren't, I know) you will admit that this is true of you; you exist in the hope that one day things will be sufficiently smoothed out for you to begin to live. That is just where you differ from the man whose brain is his hobby. His daily routine consists in a meditation in the following vein: "This day is before me. The circumstances of this day are my environment; they are the material out of which, by means of my brain, I have to live and be happy and to refrain from causing unhappiness in other people. It is the business of my brain to make use of *this* material. My brain is in its box for that sole purpose. Not to-morrow! Not next year! Not when I have made my fortune! Not when my sick child is out of danger! Not when my wife has returned to her senses! Not when my salary is raised! Not when I have passed that examination! Not when my indigestion is better! But *now!* To-day, exactly as to-day is! The facts of to-day, which in my unregeneracy I regarded primarily as anxieties, nuisances, impediments, I now regard as so much raw material from which my brain has to weave a tissue of life that is comely."

And then he foresees the day as well as he can. His experience teaches him where he will have difficulty, and he administers to his brain the lessons of which it will have most need. He carefully looks the machine over, and arranges it specially for the sort of road which he knows that it will have to traverse. And especially he readjusts his point of view, for his point of view is continually getting wrong. He is continually seeing worries where he ought to see material. He may notice, for instance, a patch on the back of his head, and he wonders whether it is the result of age or of disease, or whether it has always been there. And his wife tells him he must call at the chemist's and satisfy himself at once. Frightful nuisance! Age! The endless trouble of a capillary complaint! Calling at the chemist's will make him late at the office! etc., etc. But then his skilled, efficient brain intervenes: "What peculiarly interesting material this mean and petty circumstance yields for the practice of philosophy and right living!" And again: "Is *this* to ruffle you, O my soul? Will it serve any end whatever that I should buzz nervously round this circumstance instead of attending to my usual business?"

I give this as an example of the necessity of adjusting the point of view, and of the manner in which a brain habituated by suitable concentration to correct thinking will come to the rescue in unexpected contingencies. Naturally it will work with greater certainty in the manipulation of difficulties that are expected, that can be "seen coming"; and preparation for the expected is, fortunately, preparation for the unexpected. The man who commences his day by a steady contemplation of the dangers which the next sixteen hours are likely to furnish, and by arming himself specially against those dangers, has thereby armed himself, though to a less extent, against dangers which he did not dream of. But the routine must be fairly elastic. It may be necessary to commence several days in succession—for a week or for months, even—with disciplining the brain in one particular detail, to the temporary neglect of other matters. It is astonishing how you can weed every inch of a garden path and keep it in the most meticulous order, and then one morning find in the very middle of it a lusty, full-grown plant whose roots are positively mortised in granite! All gardeners are familiar with such discoveries.

But a similar discovery, though it entails hard labour on him, will not disgust the man whose hobby is his brain. For the discovery in itself is part of the material out of which he has to live.

If a man is to turn everything whatsoever into his own calm, dignity, and happiness, he must make this use even of his own failures. He must look at them as phenomena of the brain in that box, and cheerfully set about taking measures to prevent their repetition. All that happens to him, success or check, will but serve to increase his interest in the contents of that box. I seem to hear you saying: "And a fine egotist he'll be!" Well, he'll be the right sort of egotist. The average man is not half enough of an egotist. If egotism means a terrific interest in one's self, egotism is absolutely essential to efficient living. There is no getting away from that. But if egotism means selfishness, the serious student of the craft of daily living will not be an egotist for more than about a year. In a year he will have proved the ineptitude of egotism.

XIII

SUCCESS AND FAILURE

I am sadly aware that these brief chapters will be apt to convey, especially to the trustful and enthusiastic reader, a false impression; the impression of simplicity; and that when experience has roughly corrected this impression, the said reader, unless he is most solemnly warned, may abandon the entire enterprise in a fit of disgust, and for ever afterwards maintain a cynical and impolite attitude towards all theories of controlling the human machine. Now, the enterprise is not a simple one. It is based on one simple principle—the conscious discipline of the brain by selected habits of thought—but it is just about as complicated as anything well could be. Advanced golf is child's play compared to it. The man who briefly says to himself: "I will get up at 8, and from 8.30 to 9 I will examine and control my brain, and so my life will at once be instantly improved out of recognition"—that man is destined to unpleasant surprises. Progress will be slow. Progress may appear to be quite rapid at first, and then a period of futility may set in, and the would-be vanquisher of his brain may suffer a series of the most deadly defeats. And in his pessimism he may imagine that all his pains have gone for nothing, and that the unserious loungers in exhibition gardens and readers of novels in parlours are in the right of it after all. He may even feel rather ashamed of himself for having been, as he thinks, taken in by specious promises, like the purchaser of a quack medicine.

The conviction that great effort has been made and no progress achieved is the chief of the dangers that affront the beginner in machine-tending. It is, I will assert positively, in every case a conviction unjustified by the facts, and usually it is the mere result of reaction after fatigue, encouraged by the instinct for laziness. I do not think it will survive an impartial examination; but I know that a man, in order to find an excuse for abandoning further effort, is capable of convincing himself that past effort has yielded no fruit at all. So curious is the human machine. I beg every student of himself to consider this remark with all the intellectual honesty at his disposal. It is a grave warning.

When the machine-tender observes that he is frequently changing his point of view; when he notices that what he regarded as the kernel of the difficulty yesterday has sunk to a triviality to-day, being replaced by a fresh phenomenon; when he arises one morning and by means of a new, unexpected glimpse into the recesses of the machine perceives that hitherto he has been quite wrong and must begin again; when he wonders how on earth he could have been so blind and so stupid as not to see what now he sees; when the new vision is veiled by new disappointments and narrowed by continual reservations; when he is overwhelmed by the complexity of his undertaking—then let him unhearten himself, for he is succeeding. The history of success in any art—and machine-tending is an art—is a history of recommencements, of the dispersal and reforming of doubts, of an ever-increasing conception of the extent of the territory unconquered, and an ever-decreasing conception of the extent of the territory conquered.

It is remarkable that, though no enterprise could possibly present more diverse and changeful excitements than the mastering of the brain, the second great danger which threatens its ultimate success is nothing but a mere drying-up of enthusiasm for it! One would have thought that in an affair which concerned him so nearly, in an affair whose results might be in a very strict sense vital to him, in an affair upon which his happiness and misery might certainly turn, a man would not weary from sheer tedium. Nevertheless, it is so. Again and again I have noticed the abandonment, temporary or permanent, of this mighty and thrilling enterprise from simple lack of interest. And I imagine that, in practically all cases save those in which an exceptional original force of will renders the enterprise scarcely necessary, the interest in it will languish unless it is regularly nourished from without. Now, the interest in it cannot be nourished from without by means of conversation with other brain-tamers. There are certain things which may not be discussed by sanely organised people; and this is one. The affair is too intimate, and it is also too moral. Even after only a few minutes' vocalisation on this subject a deadly infection seems to creep into the air— the infection of priggishness. (Or am I mistaken, and do I fancy this horror? No; I cannot believe that I am mistaken.)

Hence the nourishment must be obtained by reading; a little reading every day. I suppose there are some thousands of authors who have written with more or less sincerity on the management of the human machine. But the two which, for me, stand out easily above all the rest are Marcus Aurelius Antoninus and Epictetus. Not much has been discovered since their time. "The perfecting of life is a power residing in the soul," wrote Marcus Aurelius in the ninth book of "To Himself," over seventeen hundred years ago. Marcus Aurelius is assuredly regarded as the greatest of writers in the human machine school, and not to read him daily is considered by many to be a bad habit. As a confession his work stands alone. But as a practical "Bradshaw" of existence, I would put the discourses of Epictetus before M. Aurelius. Epictetus is grosser; he will call you a blockhead as soon as look at you; he is witty, he is even humorous, and he never wanders far away from the incidents of daily life. He is brimming over with actuality for readers of the year 1908. He was a freed slave. M. Aurelius was an Emperor, and he had the morbidity from which all emperors must suffer. A finer soul than Epictetus, he is not, in my view, so useful a companion. Not all of us can breathe freely in his atmosphere. Nevertheless, he is of course to be read, and re-read continually. When you have gone through Epictetus—a single page or paragraph per day, well masticated and digested, suffices—you can go through M. Aurelius, and then you can return to Epictetus, and so on, morning by morning, or night by night, till your life's end. And they will conserve your interest in yourself.

In the matter of concentration, I hesitate to recommend Mrs. Annie Besant's "Thought Power," and yet I should be possibly unjust if I did not recommend it, having regard to its immense influence on myself. It is not one of the best books of this astounding woman. It is addressed to theosophists, and can only be completely understood in the light of theosophistic doctrines. (To grasp it all I found myself obliged to study a much larger work dealing with theosophy as a whole.) It contains an appreciable quantity of what strikes me as feeble sentimentalism, and also a lot of sheer dogma. But it is the least unsatisfactory manual of the brain that I have met with. And if the profane reader ignores all that is either Greek or twaddle to him, there will yet remain for his advantage a vast amount of very sound information and advice. All these three books are cheap.

XIV

A Man and His Environment

I now come to an entirely different aspect of the whole subject. Hitherto I have dealt with the human machine as a contrivance for adapting the man to his environment. My aim has been to show how much depends on the machine and how little depends on the environment, and that the essential business of the machine is to utilise, for making the stuff of life, the particular environment in which it happens to find itself—and no other! All this, however, does not imply that one must accept, fatalistically and permanently and passively, any preposterous environment into which destiny has chanced to throw us. If we carry far enough the discipline of our brains, we can, no doubt, arrive at surprisingly good results in no matter what environment. But it would not be "right reason" to expend an excessive amount of will-power on brain-discipline when a slighter effort in a different direction would produce consequences more felicitous. A man whom fate had pitched into a canal might accomplish miracles in the way of rendering himself amphibian; he might stagger the world by the spectacle of his philosophy under amazing difficulties; people might pay sixpence a head to come and see him; but he would be less of a nincompoop if he climbed out and arranged to live definitely on the bank.

The advantage of an adequate study of the control of the machine, such as I have outlined, is that it enables the student to judge, with some certainty, whether the unsatisfactoriness of his life is caused by a disordered machine or by an environment for which the machine is, in its fundamental construction,

unsuitable. It does help him to decide justly whether, in the case
of a grave difference between them, he, or the rest of the universe, is in the wrong. And also, if he decides that he is not in
the wrong, it helps him to choose a new environment, or to
modify the old, upon some scientific principle. The vast majority of people never know, with any precision, why they are dissatisfied with their sojourn on this planet. They make long and
fatiguing excursions in search of precious materials which all the
while are concealed in their own breasts. They don't know what
they want; they only know that they want something. Or, if they
contrive to settle in their own minds what they do want, a hundred to one the obtaining of it will leave them just as far off contentment as they were at the beginning! This is a matter of daily
observation: that people are frantically engaged in attempting to
get hold of things which, by universal experience, are hideously
disappointing to those who have obtained possession of them.
And still the struggle goes on, and probably will go on. All
because brains are lying idle! "It is no trifle that is at stake," said
Epictetus as to the question of control of instinct by reason. "*It
means, Are you in your senses or are you not?*" In this significance, indubitably the vast majority of people are not in their
senses; otherwise they would not behave as they do, so vaguely,
so happy-go-luckily, so blindly. But the man whose brain is in
working order emphatically *is* in his senses.

And when a man, by means of the efficiency of his brain, has
put his reason in definite command over his instincts, he at once
sees things in a truer perspective than was before possible, and
therefore he is able to set a just value upon the various parts
which go to make up his environment. If, for instance, he lives
in London, and is aware of constant friction, he will be led to
examine the claims of London as a Mecca for intelligent persons. He may say to himself: "There is something wrong, and
the seat of trouble is not in the machine. London compels me to
tolerate dirt, darkness, ugliness, strain, tedious daily journey-
ings, and general expensiveness. What does London give me in
exchange?" And he may decide that, as London offers him nothing special in exchange except the glamour of London and an
occasional seat at a good concert or a bad play, he may get a

better return for his expenditure of brains, nerves, and money in the provinces. He may perceive, with a certain French novelist, that "most people of truly distinguished mind prefer the provinces." And he may then actually, in obedience to reason, quit the deceptions of London with a tranquil heart, sure of his diagnosis. Whereas a man who had not devoted much time to the care of his mental machinery could not screw himself up to the step, partly from lack of resolution, and partly because he had never examined the sources of his unhappiness. A man who, not having full control of his machine, is consistently dissatisfied with his existence, is like a man who is being secretly poisoned and cannot decide with what or by whom. And so he has no middle course between absolute starvation and a continuance of poisoning.

As with the environment of place, so with the environment of individuals. Most friction between individuals is avoidable friction; sometimes, however, friction springs from such deep causes that no skill in the machine can do away with it. But how is the man whose brain is not in command of his existence to judge whether the unpleasantness can be cured or not, whether it arises in himself or in the other? He simply cannot judge. Whereas a man who keeps his brain for use and not for idle amusement will, when he sees that friction persists in spite of his brain, be so clearly impressed by the advisability of separation as the sole cure that he will steel himself to the effort necessary for a separation. One of the chief advantages of an efficient brain is that an efficient brain is capable of acting with firmness and resolution, partly, of course, because it has been toned up, but more because its operations are not confused by the interference of mere instincts.

Thirdly, there is the environment of one's general purpose in life, which is, I feel convinced, far more often hopelessly wrong and futile than either the environment of situation or the environment of individuals. I will be bold enough to say that quite seventy per cent of ambition is never realised at all, and that ninety-nine per cent of all realised ambition is fruitless. In other words, that a gigantic sacrifice of the present to the future is always going on. And here again the utility of brain-discipline is

most strikingly shown. A man whose first business it is every day
to concentrate his mind on the proper performance of that particular day, must necessarily conserve his interest in the present.
It is impossible that his perspective should become so warped
that he will devote, say, fifty-five years of his career to problem-
atical preparations for his comfort and his glory during the final
ten years. A man whose brain is his servant, and not his lady-
help or his pet dog, will be in receipt of such daily content and
satisfaction that he will early ask himself the question: "As for
this ambition that is eating away my hours, what will it give me
that I have not already got?" Further, the steady development of
interest in the hobby (call it!) of common-sense daily living will
act as an automatic test of any ambition. If an ambition survives
and flourishes on the top of that daily cultivation of the machine,
then the owner of the ambition may be sure that it is a genuine
and an invincible ambition, and he may pursue it in full faith; his
developed care for the present will prevent him from making his
ambition an altar on which the whole of the present is to be
offered up.

I shall be told that I want to do away with ambition, and that
ambition is the great motive-power of existence, and that therefore I am an enemy of society and the truth is not in me. But I
do not want to do away with ambition. What I say is that current
ambitions usually result in disappointment, that they usually
mean the complete distortion of a life. This is an incontestable
fact, and the reason of it is that ambitions are chosen either
without knowledge of their real value or without knowledge of
what they will cost. A disciplined brain will at once show the
unnecessariness of most ambitions, and will ensure that the
remainder shall be conducted with reason. It will also convince
its possessor that the ambition to live strictly according to the
highest common sense during the next twenty-four hours is an
ambition that needs a lot of beating.

XV

L. S. D.

Anybody who really wishes to talk simple truth about money at the present time is confronted by a very serious practical difficulty. He must put himself in opposition to the overwhelming body of public opinion, and resign himself to being regarded either as a *poseur*, a crank, or a fool. The public is in search of happiness now, as it was a million years ago. Money is not the principal factor in happiness. It may be argued whether, as a factor in happiness, money is of twentieth-rate importance or fiftieth-rate importance. But it cannot be argued whether money, in point of fact, does or does not of itself bring happiness. There can be no doubt whatever that money does not bring happiness. Yet, in face of this incontrovertible and universal truth, the whole public behaves exactly as if money were the sole or the principal preliminary to happiness. The public does not reason, and it will not listen to reason; its blood is up in the money-hunt, and the philosopher might as well expostulate with an earthquake as try to take that public by the button-hole and explain. If a man sacrifices his interest under the will of some dead social tyrant in order to marry whom he wishes, if an English minister of religion declines twenty-five thousand dollars a year to go into exile and preach to New York millionaires, the phenomenon is genuinely held to be so astounding that it at once flies right round the world in the form of exclamatory newspaper articles! In an age when such an attitude towards money is sincere, it is positively dangerous—I doubt if it may not be harmful—to persist with loud obstinacy that money, instead of being the greatest, is the least thing in the world. In times of high military excitement a man may be ostracised if not

117

lynched for uttering opinions which everybody will accept as truisms a couple of years later, and thus the wise philosopher holds his tongue—lest it should be cut out. So at the zenith of a period when the possession of money in absurd masses is an infallible means to the general respect, I have no intention either of preaching or of practising quite all that I privately believe in the matter of riches.

It was not always thus. Though there have been previous ages as lustful for wealth and ostentation as our own, there have also been ages when money-getting and millionaire-envying were not the sole preoccupations of the average man. And such an age will undoubtedly succeed to ours. Few things would surprise me less, in social life, than the upspringing of some anti-luxury movement, the formation of some league or guild among the middling classes (where alone intellect is to be found in quantity), the members of which would bind themselves to stand aloof from all the great, silly, banal, ugly, and tedious *luxe*-activities of the time, and not to spend more than a certain sum per annum on eating, drinking, covering their bodies, and being moved about like parcels from one spot of the earth's surface to another. Such a movement would, and will, help towards the formation of an opinion which would condemn lavish expenditure on personal satisfactions as bad form. However, the shareholders of grand hotels, restaurants, and race-courses of all sorts, together with popular singers and barristers, etc., need feel no immediate alarm. The movement is not yet.

As touching the effect of money on the efficient ordering of the human machine, there is happily no necessity to inform those who have begun to interest themselves in the conduct of their own brains that money counts for very little in that paramount affair. Nothing that really helps towards perfection costs more than is within the means of every person who reads these pages. The expenses connected with daily meditation, with the building-up of mental habits, with the practice of self-control and of cheerfulness, with the enthronement of reason over the rabble of primeval instincts—these expenses are really, you know, trifling. And whether you get that well-deserved rise of a pound a week or whether you don't, you may anyhow go ahead with the machine; it isn't a motor-car, though I started by comparing it to one. And even when, having to a certain extent mastered, through sensible management of the machine, the art of achieving a daily content and dignity, you come to the embroidery of life—even the best embroidery of life is not absolutely ruinous. Meat may go up in price—it has done—but books won't. Admission to picture galleries and concerts and so forth will remain quite low. The views from Richmond Hill or Hindhead, or along Pall Mall at sunset, the smell of the earth, the taste of fruit and of kisses—these things are unaffected by the machinations of trusts and the hysteria of stock exchanges. Travel, which after books is the finest of all embroideries (and which is not to be valued by the mile but by the quality), is decidedly cheaper than ever it was. All that is required is ingenuity in one's expenditure. And much ingenuity with a little money is vastly more profitable and amusing than much money without ingenuity.

And all the while as you read this you are saying, with your impatient sneer: "It's all very well; it's all very fine talking, *but* . . ." In brief, you are not convinced. You cannot deracinate that wide-rooted dogma within your soul that more money means more joy. I regret it. But let me put one question, and let me ask you to answer it honestly. Your financial means are greater now than they used to be. Are you happier or less discontented than you used to be? Taking your existence day by day, hour by hour, judging it by the mysterious *feel* (in the chest) of responsibilities, worries, positive joys and satisfactions, are you genuinely happier than you used to be?

I do not wish to be misunderstood. The financial question cannot be ignored. If it is true that money does not bring happiness, it is no less true that the lack of money induces a state of affairs in which efficient living becomes doubly difficult. These two propositions, superficially perhaps self-contradictory, are not really so. A modest income suffices for the fullest realisation of the Ego in terms of content and dignity; but you must live within it. You cannot righteously ignore money. A man, for instance, who cultivates himself and instructs a family of daughters in everything except the ability to earn their own livelihood, and then has the impudence to die suddenly without leaving a penny—that man is a scoundrel. Ninety—or should I say ninety-nine?—per cent of all those anxieties which render proper living almost impossible are caused by the habit of walking on the edge of one's income as one might walk on the edge of a precipice. The majority of Englishmen have some financial worry or other continually, everlastingly at the back of their minds. The sacrifice necessary to abolish this condition of things is more apparent than real. All spending is a matter of habit.

Speaking generally, a man can contrive, out of an extremely modest income, to have all that he needs—unless he needs the esteem of snobs. Habit may, and habit usually does, make it just as difficult to keep a family on two thousand a year as on two hundred. I suppose that for the majority of men the suspension of income for a single month would mean either bankruptcy, the usurer, or acute inconvenience. Impossible, under such circumstances, to be in full and independent possession of one's immortal soul! Hence I should be inclined to say that the first preliminary to a proper control of the machine is the habit of spending decidedly less than one earns or receives. The veriest automaton of a clerk ought to have the wherewithal of a whole year as a shield against the caprices of his employer. It would be as reasonable to expect the inhabitants of an unfortified city in the midst of a plain occupied by a hostile army to apply themselves successfully to the study of logarithms or metaphysics, as to expect a man without a year's income in his safe to apply himself successfully to the true art of living.

And the whole secret of relative freedom from financial anxiety lies not in income, but in expenditure. I am ashamed to utter this antique platitude. But, like most aphorisms of unassailable wisdom, it is completely ignored. You say, of course, that it is not easy to leave a margin between your expenditure and your present income. I know it. I fraternally shake your hand. Still, it is, in most cases, far easier to lessen one's expenditure than to increase one's income without increasing one's expenditure. The alternative is before you. However you decide, be assured that the foundation of philosophy is a margin, and that the margin can always be had.

XVI

Reason, Reason!

In conclusion, I must insist upon several results of what I may call the "intensive culture" of the reason. The brain will not only grow more effectively powerful in the departments of life where the brain is supposed specially to work, but it will also enlarge the circle of its activities. It will assuredly interfere in everything. The student of himself must necessarily conduct his existence more and more according to the views of his brain. This will be most salutary and agreeable both for himself and for the rest of the world. You object. You say it will be a pity when mankind refers everything to reason. You talk about the heart. You envisage an entirely reasonable existence as a harsh and callous existence. Not so. When the reason and the heart come into conflict the heart is invariably wrong. I do not say that the reason is always entirely right, but I do say that it is always less wrong than the heart. The empire of the reason is not universal, but within its empire reason is supreme, and if other forces challenge it on its own soil they must take the consequences. Nearly always, when the heart opposes the brain, the heart is merely a pretty name which we give to our idleness and our egotism.

We pass along the Strand and see a respectable young widow standing in the gutter, with a baby in her arms and a couple of boxes of matches in one hand. We know she is a widow because of her weeds, and we know she is respectable by her clothes. We know she is not begging because she is selling matches. The sight of her in the gutter pains our heart. Our heart weeps and gives the woman a penny in exchange for a halfpenny box of matches, and the pain of our heart is thereby assuaged. Our heart has performed a good action. But later on our reason (unfortunately asleep at the moment) wakes up and says: "That baby was hired; the weeds and matches merely a dodge. The whole affair was a spectacle got up to extract money from a fool like you. It is as mechanical as a penny in the slot. Instead of relieving distress you have simply helped to perpetuate an infamous system. You ought to know that you can't do good in that offhand way." The heart gives pennies in the street. The brain runs the Charity Organisation Society. Of course, to give pennies in the street is much less trouble than to run the C.O.S. As a method of producing a quick, inexpensive, and pleasing effect on one's egotism the C.O.S. is simply not in it with this dodge of giving pennies at random, without inquiry. Only—which of the two devices ought to be accused of harshness and callousness? Which of them is truly kind? I bring forward the respectable young widow as a sample case of the Heart *v.* Brain conflict. All other cases are the same. The brain is always more kind than the heart; the brain is always more willing than the heart to put itself to a great deal of trouble for a very little reward; the brain always does the difficult, unselfish thing, and the heart always does the facile, showy thing. Naturally the result of the brain's activity on society is always more advantageous than the result of the heart's activity.

Another point. I have tried to show that, if the reason is put in command of the feelings, it is impossible to assume an attitude of blame towards any person whatsoever for any act whatsoever. The habit of blaming must depart absolutely. It is no argument against this statement that it involves anarchy and the demolition of society. Even if it did (which emphatically it does not), that would not affect its truth. All great truths have been assailed on the ground that to accept them meant the end of everything. As if that mattered! As I make no claim to be the discoverer of this truth I have no hesitation in announcing it to be one of the most important truths that the world has yet to learn. However, the real reason why many people object to this truth is not because they think it involves the utter demolition of society (fear of the utter demolition of society never stopped anyone from doing or believing anything, and never will), but because they say to themselves that if they can't blame they can't praise. And they do so like praising! If they are so desperately fond of praising, it is a pity that they don't praise a little more! There can be no doubt that the average man blames much more than he praises. His instinct is to blame. If he is satisfied he says nothing; if he is not, he most illogically kicks up a row. So that even if the suppression of blame involved the suppression of praise the change would certainly be a change for the better. But I can perceive no reason why the suppression of blame should involve the suppression of praise. On the contrary, I think that the habit of praising should be fostered. (I do not suggest the occasional use of trowels, but the regular use of salt-spoons.) Anyhow, the triumph of the brain over the natural instincts (in an ideally organised man the brain and the natural instincts will never have even a tiff) always means the ultimate triumph of kindness.

And, further, the culture of the brain, the constant disciplinary exercise of the reasoning faculty, means the diminution of misdeeds. (Do not imagine I am hinting that you are on the verge of murdering your wife or breaking into your neighbour's house. Although you personally are guiltless, there is a good deal of sin still committed in your immediate vicinity.) Said Balzac in "La Cousine Bette," "A crime is in the first instance a defect of reasoning powers." In the appreciation of this truth, Marcus Aurelius was, as usual, a bit beforehand with Balzac. M. Aurelius said, "No soul wilfully misses truth." And Epictetus had come to the same conclusion before M. Aurelius, and Plato before Epictetus. All wrongdoing is done in the sincere belief that it is the best thing to do. Whatever sin a man does he does either for his own benefit or for the benefit of society. At the moment of doing it he is convinced that it is the only thing to do. He is mistaken. And he is mistaken because his brain has been unequal to the task of reasoning the matter out. Passion (the heart) is responsible for all crimes. Indeed, crime is simply a convenient monosyllable which we apply to what happens when the brain and the heart come into conflict and the brain is defeated. That transaction of the matches was a crime, you know.

Lastly, the culture of the brain must result in the habit of originally examining all the phenomena of life and conduct, to see
what they really are, and to what they lead. The heart hates
progress, because the dear old thing always wants to do as has
always been done. The heart is convinced that custom is a
virtue. The heart of the dirty working man rebels when the State
insists that he shall be clean, for no other reason than that it is
his custom to be dirty. Useless to tell his heart that, clean, he will
live longer! He has been dirty and he will be. The brain alone is
the enemy of prejudice and precedent, which alone are the enemies of progress. And this habit of originally examining phenomena is perhaps the greatest factor that goes to the making of
personal dignity; for it fosters reliance on one's self and courage
to accept the consequences of the act of reasoning. Reason is
the basis of personal dignity.

I finish. I have said nothing of the modifications which the
constant use of the brain will bring about in the *general values
of existence*. Modifications slow and subtle, but tremendous!
The persevering will discover them. It will happen to the persevering that their whole lives are changed—texture and colour,
too! Naught will happen to those who do not persevere.

A CATALOG OF SELECTED DOVER
BOOKS IN ALL FIELDS OF INTEREST

CONCERNING THE SPIRITUAL IN ART, Wassily Kandinsky. Pioneering work by father of abstract art. Thoughts on color theory, nature of art. Analysis of earlier masters. 12 illustrations. 80pp. of text. 5⅜ x 8½.   0-486-23411-8

CELTIC ART: The Methods of Construction, George Bain. Simple geometric techniques for making Celtic interlacements, spirals, Kells-type initials, animals, humans, etc. Over 500 illustrations. 160pp. 9 x 12. (Available in U.S. only.)   0-486-22923-8

AN ATLAS OF ANATOMY FOR ARTISTS, Fritz Schider. Most thorough reference work on art anatomy in the world. Hundreds of illustrations, including selections from works by Vesalius, Leonardo, Goya, Ingres, Michelangelo, others. 593 illustrations. 192pp. 7⅞ x 10¼.   0-486-20241-0

CELTIC HAND STROKE-BY-STROKE (Irish Half-Uncial from "The Book of Kells"): An Arthur Baker Calligraphy Manual, Arthur Baker. Complete guide to creating each letter of the alphabet in distinctive Celtic manner. Covers hand position, strokes, pens, inks, paper, more. Illustrated. 48pp. 8¼ x 11.   0-486-24336-2

EASY ORIGAMI, John Montroll. Charming collection of 32 projects (hat, cup, pelican, piano, swan, many more) specially designed for the novice origami hobbyist. Clearly illustrated easy-to-follow instructions insure that even beginning papercrafters will achieve successful results. 48pp. 8¼ x 11.   0-486-27298-2

BLOOMINGDALE'S ILLUSTRATED 1886 CATALOG: Fashions, Dry Goods and Housewares, Bloomingdale Brothers. Famed merchants' extremely rare catalog depicting about 1,700 products: clothing, housewares, firearms, dry goods, jewelry, more. Invaluable for dating, identifying vintage items. Also, copyright-free graphics for artists, designers. Co-published with Henry Ford Museum & Greenfield Village. 160pp. 8¼ x 11.   0-486-25780-0

THE ART OF WORLDLY WISDOM, Baltasar Gracian. "Think with the few and speak with the many," "Friends are a second existence," and "Be able to forget" are among this 1637 volume's 300 pithy maxims. A perfect source of mental and spiritual refreshment, it can be opened at random and appreciated either in brief or at length. 128pp. 5⅜ x 8½.   0-486-44034-6

JOHNSON'S DICTIONARY: A Modern Selection, Samuel Johnson (E. L. McAdam and George Milne, eds.). This modern version reduces the original 1755 edition's 2,300 pages of definitions and literary examples to a more manageable length, retaining the verbal pleasure and historical curiosity of the original. 480pp. 5⁵⁄₁₆ x 8¼.   0-486-44089-3

ADVENTURES OF HUCKLEBERRY FINN, Mark Twain, Illustrated by E. W. Kemble. A work of eternal richness and complexity, a source of ongoing critical debate, and a literary landmark, Twain's 1885 masterpiece about a barefoot boy's journey of self-discovery has enthralled readers around the world. This handsome clothbound reproduction of the first edition features all 174 of the original black-and-white illustrations. 368pp. 5⅜ x 8½.   0-486-44322-1

STICKLEY CRAFTSMAN FURNITURE CATALOGS, Gustav Stickley and L. & J. G. Stickley. Beautiful, functional furniture in two authentic catalogs from 1910. 594 illustrations, including 277 photos, show settles, rockers, armchairs, reclining chairs, bookcases, desks, tables. 183pp. 6½ x 9¼. 0-486-23838-5

AMERICAN LOCOMOTIVES IN HISTORIC PHOTOGRAPHS: 1858 to 1949, Ron Ziel (ed.). A rare collection of 126 meticulously detailed official photographs, called "builder portraits," of American locomotives that majestically chronicle the rise of steam locomotive power in America. Introduction. Detailed captions. xi+ 129pp. 9 x 12. 0-486-27393-8

AMERICA'S LIGHTHOUSES: An Illustrated History, Francis Ross Holland, Jr. Delightfully written, profusely illustrated fact-filled survey of over 200 American lighthouses since 1716. History, anecdotes, technological advances, more. 240pp. 8 x 10¾. 0-486-25576-X

TOWARDS A NEW ARCHITECTURE, Le Corbusier. Pioneering manifesto by founder of "International School." Technical and aesthetic theories, views of industry, economics, relation of form to function, "mass-production split" and much more. Profusely illustrated. 320pp. 6⅛ x 9¼. (Available in U.S. only.) 0-486-25023-7

HOW THE OTHER HALF LIVES, Jacob Riis. Famous journalistic record, exposing poverty and degradation of New York slums around 1900, by major social reformer. 100 striking and influential photographs. 233pp. 10 x 7⅞. 0-486-22012-5

FRUIT KEY AND TWIG KEY TO TREES AND SHRUBS, William M. Harlow. One of the handiest and most widely used identification aids. Fruit key covers 120 deciduous and evergreen species; twig key 160 deciduous species. Easily used. Over 300 photographs. 126pp. 5⅜ x 8½. 0-486-20511-8

COMMON BIRD SONGS, Dr. Donald J. Borror. Songs of 60 most common U.S. birds: robins, sparrows, cardinals, bluejays, finches, more—arranged in order of increasing complexity. Up to 9 variations of songs of each species. Cassette and manual 0-486-99911-4

ORCHIDS AS HOUSE PLANTS, Rebecca Tyson Northen. Grow cattleyas and many other kinds of orchids—in a window, in a case, or under artificial light. 63 illustrations. 148pp. 5⅜ x 8½. 0-486-23261-1

MONSTER MAZES, Dave Phillips. Masterful mazes at four levels of difficulty. Avoid deadly perils and evil creatures to find magical treasures. Solutions for all 32 exciting illustrated puzzles. 48pp. 8¼ x 11. 0-486-26005-4

MOZART'S DON GIOVANNI (DOVER OPERA LIBRETTO SERIES), Wolfgang Amadeus Mozart. Introduced and translated by Ellen H. Bleiler. Standard Italian libretto, with complete English translation. Convenient and thoroughly portable—an ideal companion for reading along with a recording or the performance itself. Introduction. List of characters. Plot summary. 121pp. 5¼ x 8½. 0-486-24944-1

FRANK LLOYD WRIGHT'S DANA HOUSE, Donald Hoffmann. Pictorial essay of residential masterpiece with over 160 interior and exterior photos, plans, elevations, sketches and studies. 128pp. 9¼ x 10¾. 0-486-29120-0

THE CLARINET AND CLARINET PLAYING, David Pino. Lively, comprehensive work features suggestions about technique, musicianship, and musical interpretation, as well as guidelines for teaching, making your own reeds, and preparing for public performance. Includes an intriguing look at clarinet history. "A godsend," *The Clarinet,* Journal of the International Clarinet Society. Appendixes. 7 illus. 320pp. 5⅜ x 8½. 0-486-40270-3

HOLLYWOOD GLAMOR PORTRAITS, John Kobal (ed.). 145 photos from 1926-49. Harlow, Gable, Bogart, Bacall; 94 stars in all. Full background on photographers, technical aspects. 160pp. 8⅜ x 11¼. 0-486-23352-9

THE RAVEN AND OTHER FAVORITE POEMS, Edgar Allan Poe. Over 40 of the author's most memorable poems: "The Bells," "Ulalume," "Israfel," "To Helen," "The Conqueror Worm," "Eldorado," "Annabel Lee," many more. Alphabetic lists of titles and first lines. 64pp. 5³⁄₁₆ x 8¼. 0-486-26685-0

PERSONAL MEMOIRS OF U. S. GRANT, Ulysses Simpson Grant. Intelligent, deeply moving firsthand account of Civil War campaigns, considered by many the finest military memoirs ever written. Includes letters, historic photographs, maps and more. 528pp. 6⅛ x 9¼. 0-486-28587-1

ANCIENT EGYPTIAN MATERIALS AND INDUSTRIES, A. Lucas and J. Harris. Fascinating, comprehensive, thoroughly documented text describes this ancient civilization's vast resources and the processes that incorporated them in daily life, including the use of animal products, building materials, cosmetics, perfumes and incense, fibers, glazed ware, glass and its manufacture, materials used in the mummification process, and much more. 544pp. 6¹⁄₈ x 9¹⁄₄. (Available in U.S. only.) 0-486-40446-3

RUSSIAN STORIES/RUSSKIE RASSKAZY: A Dual-Language Book, edited by Gleb Struve. Twelve tales by such masters as Chekhov, Tolstoy, Dostoevsky, Pushkin, others. Excellent word-for-word English translations on facing pages, plus teaching and study aids, Russian/English vocabulary, biographical/critical introductions, more. 416pp. 5⅜ x 8½. 0-486-26244-8

PHILADELPHIA THEN AND NOW: 60 Sites Photographed in the Past and Present, Kenneth Finkel and Susan Oyama. Rare photographs of City Hall, Logan Square, Independence Hall, Betsy Ross House, other landmarks juxtaposed with contemporary views. Captures changing face of historic city. Introduction. Captions. 128pp. 8¼ x 11. 0-486-25790-8

NORTH AMERICAN INDIAN LIFE: Customs and Traditions of 23 Tribes, Elsie Clews Parsons (ed.). 27 fictionalized essays by noted anthropologists examine religion, customs, government, additional facets of life among the Winnebago, Crow, Zuni, Eskimo, other tribes. 480pp. 6⅛ x 9¼. 0-486-27377-6

TECHNICAL MANUAL AND DICTIONARY OF CLASSICAL BALLET, Gail Grant. Defines, explains, comments on steps, movements, poses and concepts. 15-page pictorial section. Basic book for student, viewer. 127pp. 5⅜ x 8½. 0-486-21843-0

THE MALE AND FEMALE FIGURE IN MOTION: 60 Classic Photographic Sequences, Eadweard Muybridge. 60 true-action photographs of men and women walking, running, climbing, bending, turning, etc., reproduced from rare 19th-century masterpiece. vi + 121pp. 9 x 12. 0-486-24745-7

CATALOG OF DOVER BOOKS

ANIMALS: 1,419 Copyright-Free Illustrations of Mammals, Birds, Fish, Insects, etc., Jim Harter (ed.). Clear wood engravings present, in extremely lifelike poses, over 1,000 species of animals. One of the most extensive pictorial sourcebooks of its kind. Captions. Index. 284pp. 9 x 12. 0-486-23766-4

1001 QUESTIONS ANSWERED ABOUT THE SEASHORE, N. J. Berrill and Jacquelyn Berrill. Queries answered about dolphins, sea snails, sponges, starfish, fishes, shore birds, many others. Covers appearance, breeding, growth, feeding, much more. 305pp. 5¼ x 8¼. 0-486-23366-9

ATTRACTING BIRDS TO YOUR YARD, William J. Weber. Easy-to-follow guide offers advice on how to attract the greatest diversity of birds: birdhouses, feeders, water and waterers, much more. 96pp. 5³⁄₁₆ x 8¼. 0-486-28927-3

MEDICINAL AND OTHER USES OF NORTH AMERICAN PLANTS: A Historical Survey with Special Reference to the Eastern Indian Tribes, Charlotte Erichsen-Brown. Chronological historical citations document 500 years of usage of plants, trees, shrubs native to eastern Canada, northeastern U.S. Also complete identifying information. 343 illustrations. 544pp. 6½ x 9¼. 0-486-25951-X

STORYBOOK MAZES, Dave Phillips. 23 stories and mazes on two-page spreads: Wizard of Oz, Treasure Island, Robin Hood, etc. Solutions. 64pp. 8¼ x 11.
0-486-23628-5

AMERICAN NEGRO SONGS: 230 Folk Songs and Spirituals, Religious and Secular, John W. Work. This authoritative study traces the African influences of songs sung and played by black Americans at work, in church, and as entertainment. The author discusses the lyric significance of such songs as "Swing Low, Sweet Chariot," "John Henry," and others and offers the words and music for 230 songs. Bibliography. Index of Song Titles. 272pp. 6½ x 9¼. 0-486-40271-1

MOVIE-STAR PORTRAITS OF THE FORTIES, John Kobal (ed.). 163 glamor, studio photos of 106 stars of the 1940s: Rita Hayworth, Ava Gardner, Marlon Brando, Clark Gable, many more. 176pp. 8⅜ x 11¼. 0-486-23546-7

YEKL and THE IMPORTED BRIDEGROOM AND OTHER STORIES OF YIDDISH NEW YORK, Abraham Cahan. Film Hester Street based on *Yekl* (1896). Novel, other stories among first about Jewish immigrants on N.Y.'s East Side. 240pp. 5⅜ x 8½. 0-486-22427-9

SELECTED POEMS, Walt Whitman. Generous sampling from *Leaves of Grass*. Twenty-four poems include "I Hear America Singing," "Song of the Open Road," "I Sing the Body Electric," "When Lilacs Last in the Dooryard Bloom'd," "O Captain! My Captain!"—all reprinted from an authoritative edition. Lists of titles and first lines. 128pp. 5³⁄₁₆ x 8¼. 0-486-26878-0

SONGS OF EXPERIENCE: Facsimile Reproduction with 26 Plates in Full Color, William Blake. 26 full-color plates from a rare 1826 edition. Includes "The Tyger," "London," "Holy Thursday," and other poems. Printed text of poems. 48pp. 5¼ x 7.
0-486-24636-1

THE BEST TALES OF HOFFMANN, E. T. A. Hoffmann. 10 of Hoffmann's most important stories: "Nutcracker and the King of Mice," "The Golden Flowerpot," etc. 458pp. 5⅜ x 8½. 0-486-21793-0

THE BOOK OF TEA, Kakuzo Okakura. Minor classic of the Orient: entertaining, charming explanation, interpretation of traditional Japanese culture in terms of tea ceremony. 94pp. 5⅜ x 8½. 0-486-20070-1

FRENCH STORIES/CONTES FRANÇAIS: A Dual-Language Book, Wallace Fowlie. Ten stories by French masters, Voltaire to Camus: "Micromegas" by Voltaire; "The Atheist's Mass" by Balzac; "Minuet" by de Maupassant; "The Guest" by Camus, six more. Excellent English translations on facing pages. Also French-English vocabulary list, exercises, more. 352pp. 5⅜ x 8½. 0-486-26443-2

CHICAGO AT THE TURN OF THE CENTURY IN PHOTOGRAPHS: 122 Historic Views from the Collections of the Chicago Historical Society, Larry A. Viskochil. Rare large-format prints offer detailed views of City Hall, State Street, the Loop, Hull House, Union Station, many other landmarks, circa 1904-1913. Introduction. Captions. Maps. 144pp. 9⅜ x 12¼. 0-486-24656-6

OLD BROOKLYN IN EARLY PHOTOGRAPHS, 1865-1929, William Lee Younger. Luna Park, Gravesend race track, construction of Grand Army Plaza, moving of Hotel Brighton, etc. 157 previously unpublished photographs. 165pp. 8⅞ x 11¾. 0-486-23587-4

THE MYTHS OF THE NORTH AMERICAN INDIANS, Lewis Spence. Rich anthology of the myths and legends of the Algonquins, Iroquois, Pawnees and Sioux, prefaced by an extensive historical and ethnological commentary. 36 illustrations. 480pp. 5⅜ x 8½. 0-486-25967-6

AN ENCYCLOPEDIA OF BATTLES: Accounts of Over 1,560 Battles from 1479 B.C. to the Present, David Eggenberger. Essential details of every major battle in recorded history from the first battle of Megiddo in 1479 B.C. to Grenada in 1984. List of Battle Maps. New Appendix covering the years 1967-1984. Index. 99 illustrations. 544pp. 6½ x 9¼. 0-486-24913-1

SAILING ALONE AROUND THE WORLD, Captain Joshua Slocum. First man to sail around the world, alone, in small boat. One of great feats of seamanship told in delightful manner. 67 illustrations. 294pp. 5⅜ x 8½. 0-486-20326-3

ANARCHISM AND OTHER ESSAYS, Emma Goldman. Powerful, penetrating, prophetic essays on direct action, role of minorities, prison reform, puritan hypocrisy, violence, etc. 271pp. 5⅜ x 8½. 0-486-22484-8

MYTHS OF THE HINDUS AND BUDDHISTS, Ananda K. Coomaraswamy and Sister Nivedita. Great stories of the epics; deeds of Krishna, Shiva, taken from puranas, Vedas, folk tales; etc. 32 illustrations. 400pp. 5⅜ x 8½. 0-486-21759-0

MY BONDAGE AND MY FREEDOM, Frederick Douglass. Born a slave, Douglass became outspoken force in antislavery movement. The best of Douglass' autobiographies. Graphic description of slave life. 464pp. 5⅜ x 8½. 0-486-22457-0

FOLLOWING THE EQUATOR: A Journey Around the World, Mark Twain. Fascinating humorous account of 1897 voyage to Hawaii, Australia, India, New Zealand, etc. Ironic, bemused reports on peoples, customs, climate, flora and fauna, politics, much more. 197 illustrations. 720pp. 5⅜ x 8½. 0-486-26113-1

THE PEOPLE CALLED SHAKERS, Edward D. Andrews. Definitive study of Shakers: origins, beliefs, practices, dances, social organization, furniture and crafts, etc. 33 illustrations. 351pp. 5⅜ x 8½. 0-486-21081-2

THE MYTHS OF GREECE AND ROME, H. A. Guerber. A classic of mythology, generously illustrated, long prized for its simple, graphic, accurate retelling of the principal myths of Greece and Rome, and for its commentary on their origins and significance. With 64 illustrations by Michelangelo, Raphael, Titian, Rubens, Canova, Bernini and others. 480pp. 5⅜ x 8½. 0-486-27584-1

PSYCHOLOGY OF MUSIC, Carl E. Seashore. Classic work discusses music as a medium from psychological viewpoint. Clear treatment of physical acoustics, auditory apparatus, sound perception, development of musical skills, nature of musical feeling, host of other topics. 88 figures. 408pp. 5⅜ x 8½. 0-486-21851-1

LIFE IN ANCIENT EGYPT, Adolf Erman. Fullest, most thorough, detailed older account with much not in more recent books, domestic life, religion, magic, medicine, commerce, much more. Many illustrations reproduce tomb paintings, carvings, hieroglyphs, etc. 597pp. 5⅜ x 8½. 0-486-22632-8

SUNDIALS, Their Theory and Construction, Albert Waugh. Far and away the best, most thorough coverage of ideas, mathematics concerned, types, construction, adjusting anywhere. Simple, nontechnical treatment allows even children to build several of these dials. Over 100 illustrations. 230pp. 5⅜ x 8½. 0-486-22947-5

THEORETICAL HYDRODYNAMICS, L. M. Milne-Thomson. Classic exposition of the mathematical theory of fluid motion, applicable to both hydrodynamics and aerodynamics. Over 600 exercises. 768pp. 6⅛ x 9¼. 0-486-68970-0

OLD-TIME VIGNETTES IN FULL COLOR, Carol Belanger Grafton (ed.). Over 390 charming, often sentimental illustrations, selected from archives of Victorian graphics–pretty women posing, children playing, food, flowers, kittens and puppies, smiling cherubs, birds and butterflies, much more. All copyright-free. 48pp. 9¼ x 12¼. 0-486-27269-9

PERSPECTIVE FOR ARTISTS, Rex Vicat Cole. Depth, perspective of sky and sea, shadows, much more, not usually covered. 391 diagrams, 81 reproductions of drawings and paintings. 279pp. 5⅜ x 8½. 0-486-22487-2

DRAWING THE LIVING FIGURE, Joseph Sheppard. Innovative approach to artistic anatomy focuses on specifics of surface anatomy, rather than muscles and bones. Over 170 drawings of live models in front, back and side views, and in widely varying poses. Accompanying diagrams. 177 illustrations. Introduction. Index. 144pp. 8⅜ x11¼. 0-486-26723-7

GOTHIC AND OLD ENGLISH ALPHABETS: 100 Complete Fonts, Dan X. Solo. Add power, elegance to posters, signs, other graphics with 100 stunning copyright-free alphabets: Blackstone, Dolbey, Germania, 97 more–including many lower-case, numerals, punctuation marks. 104pp. 8⅛ x 11. 0-486-24695-7

THE BOOK OF WOOD CARVING, Charles Marshall Sayers. Finest book for beginners discusses fundamentals and offers 34 designs. "Absolutely first rate . . . well thought out and well executed."–E. J. Tangerman. 118pp. 7¾ x 10⅝. 0-486-23654-4

ILLUSTRATED CATALOG OF CIVIL WAR MILITARY GOODS: Union Army Weapons, Insignia, Uniform Accessories, and Other Equipment, Schuyler, Hartley, and Graham. Rare, profusely illustrated 1846 catalog includes Union Army uniform and dress regulations, arms and ammunition, coats, insignia, flags, swords, rifles, etc. 226 illustrations. 160pp. 9 x 12. 0-486-24939-5

WOMEN'S FASHIONS OF THE EARLY 1900s: An Unabridged Republication of "New York Fashions, 1909," National Cloak & Suit Co. Rare catalog of mail-order fashions documents women's and children's clothing styles shortly after the turn of the century. Captions offer full descriptions, prices. Invaluable resource for fashion, costume historians. Approximately 725 illustrations. 128pp. 8⅜ x 11¼. 0-486-27276-1

HOW TO DO BEADWORK, Mary White. Fundamental book on craft from simple projects to five-bead chains and woven works. 106 illustrations. 142pp. 5⅜ x 8.

0-486-20697-1

THE 1912 AND 1915 GUSTAV STICKLEY FURNITURE CATALOGS, Gustav Stickley. With over 200 detailed illustrations and descriptions, these two catalogs are essential reading and reference materials and identification guides for Stickley furniture. Captions cite materials, dimensions and prices. 112pp. 6½ x 9¼. 0-486-26676-1

EARLY AMERICAN LOCOMOTIVES, John H. White, Jr. Finest locomotive engravings from early 19th century: historical (1804–74), main-line (after 1870), special, foreign, etc. 147 plates. 142pp. 11⅜ x 8¼. 0-486-22772-3

LITTLE BOOK OF EARLY AMERICAN CRAFTS AND TRADES, Peter Stockham (ed.). 1807 children's book explains crafts and trades: baker, hatter, cooper, potter, and many others. 23 copperplate illustrations. 140pp. 4⅝ x 6.

0-486-23336-7

VICTORIAN FASHIONS AND COSTUMES FROM HARPER'S BAZAR, 1867–1898, Stella Blum (ed.). Day costumes, evening wear, sports clothes, shoes, hats, other accessories in over 1,000 detailed engravings. 320pp. 9⅜ x 12¼.

0-486-22990-4

THE LONG ISLAND RAIL ROAD IN EARLY PHOTOGRAPHS, Ron Ziel. Over 220 rare photos, informative text document origin (1844) and development of rail service on Long Island. Vintage views of early trains, locomotives, stations, passengers, crews, much more. Captions. 8⅞ x 11¾. 0-486-26301-0

VOYAGE OF THE LIBERDADE, Joshua Slocum. Great 19th-century mariner's thrilling, first-hand account of the wreck of his ship off South America, the 35-foot boat he built from the wreckage, and its remarkable voyage home. 128pp. 5⅜ x 8½.

0-486-40022-0

TEN BOOKS ON ARCHITECTURE, Vitruvius. The most important book ever written on architecture. Early Roman aesthetics, technology, classical orders, site selection, all other aspects. Morgan translation. 331pp. 5⅜ x 8½. 0-486-20645-9

THE HUMAN FIGURE IN MOTION, Eadweard Muybridge. More than 4,500 stopped-action photos, in action series, showing undraped men, women, children jumping, lying down, throwing, sitting, wrestling, carrying, etc. 390pp. 7⅞ x 10⅝.

0-486-20204-6 Clothbd.

TREES OF THE EASTERN AND CENTRAL UNITED STATES AND CANADA, William M. Harlow. Best one-volume guide to 140 trees. Full descriptions, woodlore, range, etc. Over 600 illustrations. Handy size. 288pp. 4½ x 6⅜. 0-486-20395-6

GROWING AND USING HERBS AND SPICES, Milo Miloradovich. Versatile handbook provides all the information needed for cultivation and use of all the herbs and spices available in North America. 4 illustrations. Index. Glossary. 236pp. 5⅜ x 8½.

0-486-25058-X

BIG BOOK OF MAZES AND LABYRINTHS, Walter Shepherd. 50 mazes and labyrinths in all—classical, solid, ripple, and more—in one great volume. Perfect inexpensive puzzler for clever youngsters. Full solutions. 112pp. 8⅛ x 11. 0-486-22951-3

PIANO TUNING, J. Cree Fischer. Clearest, best book for beginner, amateur. Simple repairs, raising dropped notes, tuning by easy method of flattened fifths. No previous skills needed. 4 illustrations. 201pp. 5⅜ x 8½. 0-486-23267-0

HINTS TO SINGERS, Lillian Nordica. Selecting the right teacher, developing confidence, overcoming stage fright, and many other important skills receive thoughtful discussion in this indispensible guide, written by a world-famous diva of four decades' experience. 96pp. 5⅜ x 8½. 0-486-40094-8

THE COMPLETE NONSENSE OF EDWARD LEAR, Edward Lear. All nonsense limericks, zany alphabets, Owl and Pussycat, songs, nonsense botany, etc., illustrated by Lear. Total of 320pp. 5⅜ x 8½. (Available in U.S. only.) 0-486-20167-8

VICTORIAN PARLOUR POETRY: An Annotated Anthology, Michael R. Turner. 117 gems by Longfellow, Tennyson, Browning, many lesser-known poets. "The Village Blacksmith," "Curfew Must Not Ring Tonight," "Only a Baby Small," dozens more, often difficult to find elsewhere. Index of poets, titles, first lines. xxiii + 325pp. 5⅜ x 8¼. 0-486-27044-0

DUBLINERS, James Joyce. Fifteen stories offer vivid, tightly focused observations of the lives of Dublin's poorer classes. At least one, "The Dead," is considered a masterpiece. Reprinted complete and unabridged from standard edition. 160pp. 5³⁄₁₆ x 8¼. 0-486-26870-5

GREAT WEIRD TALES: 14 Stories by Lovecraft, Blackwood, Machen and Others, S. T. Joshi (ed.). 14 spellbinding tales, including "The Sin Eater," by Fiona McLeod, "The Eye Above the Mantel," by Frank Belknap Long, as well as renowned works by R. H. Barlow, Lord Dunsany, Arthur Machen, W. C. Morrow and eight other masters of the genre. 256pp. 5⅜ x 8½. (Available in U.S. only.) 0-486-40436-6

THE BOOK OF THE SACRED MAGIC OF ABRAMELIN THE MAGE, translated by S. MacGregor Mathers. Medieval manuscript of ceremonial magic. Basic document in Aleister Crowley, Golden Dawn groups. 268pp. 5⅜ x 8½. 0-486-23211-5

THE BATTLES THAT CHANGED HISTORY, Fletcher Pratt. Eminent historian profiles 16 crucial conflicts, ancient to modern, that changed the course of civilization. 352pp. 5⅜ x 8½. 0-486-41129-X

NEW RUSSIAN ENGLISH AND ENGLISH-RUSSIAN DICTIONARY, M. A. O'Brien. This is a remarkably handy Russian dictionary, containing a surprising amount of information, including over 70,000 entries. 366pp. 4½ x 6⅛. 0-486-20208-9

NEW YORK IN THE FORTIES, Andreas Feininger. 162 brilliant photographs by the well-known photographer, formerly with *Life* magazine. Commuters, shoppers, Times Square at night, much else from city at its peak. Captions by John von Hartz. 181pp. 9¼ x 10¾. 0-486-23585-8

INDIAN SIGN LANGUAGE, William Tomkins. Over 525 signs developed by Sioux and other tribes. Written instructions and diagrams. Also 290 pictographs. 111pp. 6⅛ x 9¼. 0-486-22029-X

ANATOMY: A Complete Guide for Artists, Joseph Sheppard. A master of figure drawing shows artists how to render human anatomy convincingly. Over 460 illustrations. 224pp. 8⅜ x 11¼. 0-486-27279-6

MEDIEVAL CALLIGRAPHY: Its History and Technique, Marc Drogin. Spirited history, comprehensive instruction manual covers 13 styles (ca. 4th century through 15th). Excellent photographs; directions for duplicating medieval techniques with modern tools. 224pp. 8⅜ x 11¼. 0-486-26142-5

DRIED FLOWERS: How to Prepare Them, Sarah Whitlock and Martha Rankin. Complete instructions on how to use silica gel, meal and borax, perlite aggregate, sand and borax, glycerine and water to create attractive permanent flower arrangements. 12 illustrations. 32pp. 5⅜ x 8½. 0-486-21802-3

EASY TO MAKE BIRD FEEDERS FOR WOODWORKERS, Scott D. Campbell. Detailed, simple-to-use guide for designing, constructing, caring for and using feeders. Text, illustrations for 12 classic and contemporary designs. 96pp. 5⅜ x 8½. 0-486-25847-5

THE COMPLETE BOOK OF BIRDHOUSE CONSTRUCTION FOR WOOD-WORKERS, Scott D. Campbell. Detailed instructions, illustrations, tables. Also data on bird habitat and instinct patterns. Bibliography. 3 tables. 63 illustrations in 15 figures. 48pp. 5¼ x 8½. 0-486-24407-5

SCOTTISH WONDER TALES FROM MYTH AND LEGEND, Donald A. Mackenzie. 16 lively tales tell of giants rumbling down mountainsides, of a magic wand that turns stone pillars into warriors, of gods and goddesses, evil hags, powerful forces and more. 240pp. 5⅜ x 8½. 0-486-29677-6

THE HISTORY OF UNDERCLOTHES, C. Willett Cunnington and Phyllis Cunnington. Fascinating, well-documented survey covering six centuries of English undergarments, enhanced with over 100 illustrations: 12th-century laced-up bodice, footed long drawers (1795), 19th-century bustles, l9th-century corsets for men, Victorian "bust improvers," much more. 272pp. 5⅜ x 8¼. 0-486-27124-2

ARTS AND CRAFTS FURNITURE: The Complete Brooks Catalog of 1912, Brooks Manufacturing Co. Photos and detailed descriptions of more than 150 now very collectible furniture designs from the Arts and Crafts movement depict davenports, settees, buffets, desks, tables, chairs, bedsteads, dressers and more, all built of solid, quarter-sawed oak. Invaluable for students and enthusiasts of antiques, Americana and the decorative arts. 80pp. 6½ x 9¼. 0-486-27471-3

WILBUR AND ORVILLE: A Biography of the Wright Brothers, Fred Howard. Definitive, crisply written study tells the full story of the brothers' lives and work. A vividly written biography, unparalleled in scope and color, that also captures the spirit of an extraordinary era. 560pp. 6⅛ x 9¼. 0-486-40297-5

THE ARTS OF THE SAILOR: Knotting, Splicing and Ropework, Hervey Garrett Smith. Indispensable shipboard reference covers tools, basic knots and useful hitches; handsewing and canvas work, more. Over 100 illustrations. Delightful reading for sea lovers. 256pp. 5⅜ x 8½. 0-486-26440-8

FRANK LLOYD WRIGHT'S FALLINGWATER: The House and Its History, Second, Revised Edition, Donald Hoffmann. A total revision–both in text and illustrations–of the standard document on Fallingwater, the boldest, most personal architectural statement of Wright's mature years, updated with valuable new material from the recently opened Frank Lloyd Wright Archives. "Fascinating"–*The New York Times*. 116 illustrations. 128pp. 9¼ x 10¾. 0-486-27430-6

PHOTOGRAPHIC SKETCHBOOK OF THE CIVIL WAR, Alexander Gardner. 100 photos taken on field during the Civil War. Famous shots of Manassas Harper's Ferry, Lincoln, Richmond, slave pens, etc. 244pp. 10⅝ x 8¼. 0-486-22731-6

FIVE ACRES AND INDEPENDENCE, Maurice G. Kains. Great back-to-the-land classic explains basics of self-sufficient farming. The one book to get. 95 illustrations. 397pp. 5⅜ x 8½. 0-486-20974-1

CATALOG OF DOVER BOOKS

A MODERN HERBAL, Margaret Grieve. Much the fullest, most exact, most useful compilation of herbal material. Gigantic alphabetical encyclopedia, from aconite to zedoary, gives botanical information, medical properties, folklore, economic uses, much else. Indispensable to serious reader. 161 illustrations. 888pp. 6½ x 9¼. 2-vol. set. (Available in U.S. only.) Vol. I: 0-486-22798-7 Vol. II: 0-486-22799-5

HIDDEN TREASURE MAZE BOOK, Dave Phillips. Solve 34 challenging mazes accompanied by heroic tales of adventure. Evil dragons, people-eating plants, blood-thirsty giants, many more dangerous adversaries lurk at every twist and turn. 34 mazes, stories, solutions. 48pp. 8¼ x 11. 0-486-24566-7

LETTERS OF W. A. MOZART, Wolfgang A. Mozart. Remarkable letters show bawdy wit, humor, imagination, musical insights, contemporary musical world; includes some letters from Leopold Mozart. 276pp. 5⅜ x 8½. 0-486-22859-2

BASIC PRINCIPLES OF CLASSICAL BALLET, Agrippina Vaganova. Great Russian theoretician, teacher explains methods for teaching classical ballet. 118 illustrations. 175pp. 5⅜ x 8½. 0-486-22036-2

THE JUMPING FROG, Mark Twain. Revenge edition. The original story of The Celebrated Jumping Frog of Calaveras County, a hapless French translation, and Twain's hilarious "retranslation" from the French. 12 illustrations. 66pp. 5⅜ x 8½. 0 486 22686-7

BEST REMEMBERED POEMS, Martin Gardner (ed.). The 126 poems in this superb collection of 19th- and 20th-century British and American verse range from Shelley's "To a Skylark" to the impassioned "Renascence" of Edna St. Vincent Millay and to Edward Lear's whimsical "The Owl and the Pussycat." 224pp. 5⅜ x 8½. 0-486-27165-X

COMPLETE SONNETS, William Shakespeare. Over 150 exquisite poems deal with love, friendship, the tyranny of time, beauty's evanescence, death and other themes in language of remarkable power, precision and beauty. Glossary of archaic terms. 80pp. 5³⁄₁₆ x 8¼. 0-486-26686-9

HISTORIC HOMES OF THE AMERICAN PRESIDENTS, Second, Revised Edition, Irvin Haas. A traveler's guide to American Presidential homes, most open to the public, depicting and describing homes occupied by every American President from George Washington to George Bush. With visiting hours, admission charges, travel routes. 175 photographs. Index. 160pp. 8¼ x 11. 0-486-26751-2

THE WIT AND HUMOR OF OSCAR WILDE, Alvin Redman (ed.). More than 1,000 ripostes, paradoxes, wisecracks: Work is the curse of the drinking classes; I can resist everything except temptation; etc. 258pp. 5⅜ x 8½. 0-486-20602-5

SHAKESPEARE LEXICON AND QUOTATION DICTIONARY, Alexander Schmidt. Full definitions, locations, shades of meaning in every word in plays and poems. More than 50,000 exact quotations. 1,485pp. 6½ x 9¼. 2-vol. set. Vol. 1: 0-486-22726-X Vol. 2: 0-486-22727-8

SELECTED POEMS, Emily Dickinson. Over 100 best-known, best-loved poems by one of America's foremost poets, reprinted from authoritative early editions. No comparable edition at this price. Index of first lines. 64pp. 5³⁄₁₆ x 8¼. 0-486-26466-1

THE INSIDIOUS DR. FU-MANCHU, Sax Rohmer. The first of the popular mystery series introduces a pair of English detectives to their archnemesis, the diabolical Dr. Fu-Manchu. Flavorful atmosphere, fast-paced action, and colorful characters enliven this classic of the genre. 208pp. 5³⁄₁₆ x 8¼. 0-486-29898-1

THE MALLEUS MALEFICARUM OF KRAMER AND SPRENGER, translated by Montague Summers. Full text of most important witchhunter's "bible," used by both Catholics and Protestants. 278pp. 6⅝ x 10. 0-486-22802-9

SPANISH STORIES/CUENTOS ESPAÑOLES: A Dual-Language Book, Angel Flores (ed.). Unique format offers 13 great stories in Spanish by Cervantes, Borges, others. Faithful English translations on facing pages. 352pp. 5⅜ x 8½. 0-486-25399-6

GARDEN CITY, LONG ISLAND, IN EARLY PHOTOGRAPHS, 1869–1919, Mildred H. Smith. Handsome treasury of 118 vintage pictures, accompanied by carefully researched captions, document the Garden City Hotel fire (1899), the Vanderbilt Cup Race (1908), the first airmail flight departing from the Nassau Boulevard Aerodrome (1911), and much more. 96pp. 8⅞ x 11¾. 0-486-40669-5

OLD QUEENS, N.Y., IN EARLY PHOTOGRAPHS, Vincent F. Seyfried and William Asadorian. Over 160 rare photographs of Maspeth, Jamaica, Jackson Heights, and other areas. Vintage views of DeWitt Clinton mansion, 1939 World's Fair and more. Captions. 192pp. 8⅞ x 11. 0-486-26358-4

CAPTURED BY THE INDIANS: 15 Firsthand Accounts, 1750-1870, Frederick Drimmer. Astounding true historical accounts of grisly torture, bloody conflicts, relentless pursuits, miraculous escapes and more, by people who lived to tell the tale. 384pp. 5⅜ x 8½. 0-486-24901-8

THE WORLD'S GREAT SPEECHES (Fourth Enlarged Edition), Lewis Copeland, Lawrence W. Lamm, and Stephen J. McKenna. Nearly 300 speeches provide public speakers with a wealth of updated quotes and inspiration–from Pericles' funeral oration and William Jennings Bryan's "Cross of Gold Speech" to Malcolm X's powerful words on the Black Revolution and Earl of Spenser's tribute to his sister, Diana, Princess of Wales. 944pp. 5⅜ x 8⅜. 0-486-40903-1

THE BOOK OF THE SWORD, Sir Richard F. Burton. Great Victorian scholar/adventurer's eloquent, erudite history of the "queen of weapons"–from prehistory to early Roman Empire. Evolution and development of early swords, variations (sabre, broadsword, cutlass, scimitar, etc.), much more. 336pp. 6⅛ x 9¼. 0-486-25434-8

AUTOBIOGRAPHY: The Story of My Experiments with Truth, Mohandas K. Gandhi. Boyhood, legal studies, purification, the growth of the Satyagraha (nonviolent protest) movement. Critical, inspiring work of the man responsible for the freedom of India. 480pp. 5⅜ x 8½. (Available in U.S. only.) 0-486-24593-4

CELTIC MYTHS AND LEGENDS, T. W. Rolleston. Masterful retelling of Irish and Welsh stories and tales. Cuchulain, King Arthur, Deirdre, the Grail, many more. First paperback edition. 58 full-page illustrations. 512pp. 5⅜ x 8½. 0-486-26507-2

THE PRINCIPLES OF PSYCHOLOGY, William James. Famous long course complete, unabridged. Stream of thought, time perception, memory, experimental methods; great work decades ahead of its time. 94 figures. 1,391pp. 5⅜ x 8½. 2-vol. set.
Vol. I: 0-486-20381-6 Vol. II: 0-486-20382-4

THE WORLD AS WILL AND REPRESENTATION, Arthur Schopenhauer. Definitive English translation of Schopenhauer's life work, correcting more than 1,000 errors, omissions in earlier translations. Translated by E. F. J. Payne. Total of 1,269pp. 5⅜ x 8½. 2-vol. set. Vol. 1: 0-486-21761-2 Vol. 2: 0-486-21762-0

CATALOG OF DOVER BOOKS

MAGIC AND MYSTERY IN TIBET, Madame Alexandra David-Neel. Experiences among lamas, magicians, sages, sorcerers, Bonpa wizards. A true psychic discovery. 32 illustrations. 321pp. 5⅜ x 8½. (Available in U.S. only.)   0-486-22682-4

THE EGYPTIAN BOOK OF THE DEAD, E. A. Wallis Budge. Complete reproduction of Ani's papyrus, finest ever found. Full hieroglyphic text, interlinear transliteration, word-for-word translation, smooth translation. 533pp. 6½ x 9¼.
0-486-21866-X

HISTORIC COSTUME IN PICTURES, Braun & Schneider. Over 1,450 costumed figures in clearly detailed engravings—from dawn of civilization to end of 19th century. Captions. Many folk costumes. 256pp. 8⅜ x 11¾.   0-486-23150-X

MATHEMATICS FOR THE NONMATHEMATICIAN, Morris Kline. Detailed, college-level treatment of mathematics in cultural and historical context, with numerous exercises. Recommended Reading Lists. Tables. Numerous figures. 641pp. 5⅜ x 8½.
0-486-24823-2

PROBABILISTIC METHODS IN THE THEORY OF STRUCTURES, Isaac Elishakoff. Well-written introduction covers the elements of the theory of probability from two or more random variables, the reliability of such multivariable structures, the theory of random function, Monte Carlo methods of treating problems incapable of exact solution, and more. Examples. 502pp. 5⅜ x 8½.   0-486-40691-1

THE RIME OF THE ANCIENT MARINER, Gustave Doré, S. T. Coleridge. Doré's finest work; 34 plates capture moods, subtleties of poem. Flawless full-size reproductions printed on facing pages with authoritative text of poem. "Beautiful. Simply beautiful."—*Publisher's Weekly.* 77pp. 9¼ x 12.   0-486-22305-1

SCULPTURE: Principles and Practice, Louis Slobodkin. Step-by-step approach to clay, plaster, metals, stone; classical and modern. 253 drawings, photos. 255pp. 8⅛ x 11.
0-486-22960-2

THE INFLUENCE OF SEA POWER UPON HISTORY, 1660–1783, A. T. Mahan. Influential classic of naval history and tactics still used as text in war colleges. First paperback edition. 4 maps. 24 battle plans. 640pp. 5⅜ x 8½.   0 486 25509 3

THE STORY OF THE TITANIC AS TOLD BY ITS SURVIVORS, Jack Winocour (ed.). What it was really like. Panic, despair, shocking inefficiency, and a little heroism. More thrilling than any fictional account. 26 illustrations. 320pp. 5⅜ x 8½.
0-486-20610-6

ONE TWO THREE . . . INFINITY: Facts and Speculations of Science, George Gamow. Great physicist's fascinating, readable overview of contemporary science: number theory, relativity, fourth dimension, entropy, genes, atomic structure, much more. 128 illustrations. Index. 352pp. 5⅜ x 8½.   0-486-25664-2

DALÍ ON MODERN ART: The Cuckolds of Antiquated Modern Art, Salvador Dalí. Influential painter skewers modern art and its practitioners. Outrageous evaluations of Picasso, Cézanne, Turner, more. 15 renderings of paintings discussed. 44 calligraphic decorations by Dalí. 96pp. 5⅜ x 8½. (Available in U.S. only.)   0-486-29220-7

ANTIQUE PLAYING CARDS: A Pictorial History, Henry René D'Allemagne. Over 900 elaborate, decorative images from rare playing cards (14th–20th centuries): Bacchus, death, dancing dogs, hunting scenes, royal coats of arms, players cheating, much more. 96pp. 9¼ x 12¼.   0-486-29265-7

MAKING FURNITURE MASTERPIECES: 30 Projects with Measured Drawings, Franklin H. Gottshall. Step-by-step instructions, illustrations for constructing handsome, useful pieces, among them a Sheraton desk, Chippendale chair, Spanish desk, Queen Anne table and a William and Mary dressing mirror. 224pp. 8⅛ x 11¼.
0-486-29338-6

NORTH AMERICAN INDIAN DESIGNS FOR ARTISTS AND CRAFTSPEOPLE, Eva Wilson. Over 360 authentic copyright-free designs adapted from Navajo blankets, Hopi pottery, Sioux buffalo hides, more. Geometrics, symbolic figures, plant and animal motifs, etc. 128pp. 8⅜ x 11. (Not for sale in the United Kingdom.) 0-486-25341-4

THE FOSSIL BOOK: A Record of Prehistoric Life, Patricia V. Rich et al. Profusely illustrated definitive guide covers everything from single-celled organisms and dinosaurs to birds and mammals and the interplay between climate and man. Over 1,500 illustrations. 760pp. 7½ x 10⅛. 0-486-29371-8

VICTORIAN ARCHITECTURAL DETAILS: Designs for Over 700 Stairs, Mantels, Doors, Windows, Cornices, Porches, and Other Decorative Elements, A. J. Bicknell & Company. Everything from dormer windows and piazzas to balconies and gable ornaments. Also includes elevations and floor plans for handsome, private residences and commercial structures. 80pp. 9⅜ x 12¼. 0-486-44015-X

WESTERN ISLAMIC ARCHITECTURE: A Concise Introduction, John D. Hoag. Profusely illustrated critical appraisal compares and contrasts Islamic mosques and palaces–from Spain and Egypt to other areas in the Middle East. 139 illustrations. 128pp. 6 x 9. 0-486-43760-4

CHINESE ARCHITECTURE: A Pictorial History, Liang Ssu-ch'eng. More than 240 rare photographs and drawings depict temples, pagodas, tombs, bridges, and imperial palaces comprising much of China's architectural heritage. 152 halftones, 94 diagrams. 232pp. 10¾ x 9⅞. 0-486-43999-2

THE RENAISSANCE: Studies in Art and Poetry, Walter Pater. One of the most talked-about books of the 19th century, *The Renaissance* combines scholarship and philosophy in an innovative work of cultural criticism that examines the achievements of Botticelli, Leonardo, Michelangelo, and other artists. "The holy writ of beauty."–Oscar Wilde. 160pp. 5⅜ x 8½. 0-486-44025-7

A TREATISE ON PAINTING, Leonardo da Vinci. The great Renaissance artist's practical advice on drawing and painting techniques covers anatomy, perspective, composition, light and shadow, and color. A classic of art instruction, it features 48 drawings by Nicholas Poussin and Leon Battista Alberti. 192pp. 5⅜ x 8½.
0-486-44155-5

THE MIND OF LEONARDO DA VINCI, Edward McCurdy. More than just a biography, this classic study by a distinguished historian draws upon Leonardo's extensive writings to offer numerous demonstrations of the Renaissance master's achievements, not only in sculpture and painting, but also in music, engineering, and even experimental aviation. 384pp. 5⅜ x 8½. 0-486-44142-3

WASHINGTON IRVING'S RIP VAN WINKLE, Illustrated by Arthur Rackham. Lovely prints that established artist as a leading illustrator of the time and forever etched into the popular imagination a classic of Catskill lore. 51 full-color plates. 80pp. 8⅜ x 11. 0-486-44242-X

HENSCHE ON PAINTING, John W. Robichaux. Basic painting philosophy and methodology of a great teacher, as expounded in his famous classes and workshops on Cape Cod. 7 illustrations in color on covers. 80pp. 5⅜ x 8½. 0-486-43728-0

LIGHT AND SHADE: A Classic Approach to Three-Dimensional Drawing, Mrs. Mary P. Merrifield. Handy reference clearly demonstrates principles of light and shade by revealing effects of common daylight, sunshine, and candle or artificial light on geometrical solids. 13 plates. 64pp. 5⅜ x 8½. 0-486-44143-1

ASTROLOGY AND ASTRONOMY: A Pictorial Archive of Signs and Symbols, Ernst and Johanna Lehner. Treasure trove of stories, lore, and myth, accompanied by more than 300 rare illustrations of planets, the Milky Way, signs of the zodiac, comets, meteors, and other astronomical phenomena. 192pp. 8⅜ x 11. 0-486-43981-X

JEWELRY MAKING: Techniques for Metal, Tim McCreight. Easy-to-follow instructions and carefully executed illustrations describe tools and techniques, use of gems and enamels, wire inlay, casting, and other topics. 72 line illustrations and diagrams. 176pp. 8¼ x 10⅞. 0-486-44043-5

MAKING BIRDHOUSES: Easy and Advanced Projects, Gladstone Califf. Easy-to-follow instructions include diagrams for everything from a one-room house for bluebirds to a forty-two-room structure for purple martins. 56 plates; 4 figures. 80pp. 8¾ x 6⅜. 0-486-44183-0

LITTLE BOOK OF LOG CABINS: How to Build and Furnish Them, William S. Wicks. Handy how-to manual, with instructions and illustrations for building cabins in the Adirondack style, fireplaces, stairways, furniture, beamed ceilings, and more. 102 line drawings. 96pp. 8¾ x 6⅜. 0-486-44259-4

THE SEASONS OF AMERICA PAST, Eric Sloane. From "sugaring time" and strawberry picking to Indian summer and fall harvest, a whole year's activities described in charming prose and enhanced with 79 of the author's own illustrations. 160pp. 8¼ x 11. 0-486-44220-9

THE METROPOLIS OF TOMORROW, Hugh Ferriss. Generous, prophetic vision of the metropolis of the future, as perceived in 1929. Powerful illustrations of towering structures, wide avenues, and rooftop parks–all features in many of today's modern cities. 59 illustrations. 144pp. 8¼ x 11. 0-486-43727-2

THE PATH TO ROME, Hilaire Belloc. This 1902 memoir abounds in lively vignettes from a vanished time, recounting a pilgrimage on foot across the Alps and Apennines in order to "see all Europe which the Christian Faith has saved." 77 of the author's original line drawings complement his sparkling prose. 272pp. 5⅜ x 8½. 0-486-44001-X

THE HISTORY OF RASSELAS: Prince of Abissinia, Samuel Johnson. Distinguished English writer attacks eighteenth-century optimism and man's unrealistic estimates of what life has to offer. 112pp. 5⅜ x 8½. 0-486-44094-X

A VOYAGE TO ARCTURUS, David Lindsay. A brilliant flight of pure fancy, where wild creatures crowd the fantastic landscape and demented torturers dominate victims with their bizarre mental powers. 272pp. 5⅜ x 8½. 0-486-44198-9

Paperbound unless otherwise indicated. Available at your book dealer, online at **www.doverpublications.com**, or by writing to Dept. GI, Dover Publications, Inc., 31 East 2nd Street, Mineola, NY 11501. For current price information or for free catalogs (please indicate field of interest), write to Dover Publications or log on to **www.doverpublications.com** and see every Dover book in print. Dover publishes more than 500 books each year on science, elementary and advanced mathematics, biology, music, art, literary history, social sciences, and other areas.